LEARNING TO LET GO

LEARNING TO LET GO

When to Say Goodbye to Your Children

Carol Kuykendall

PYRANEE
BOOKS

Zondervan Publishing House
Grand Rapids, Michigan

Learning to Let Go

This is a Pyranee Book
Published by the Zondervan Publishing House
1415 Lake Drive, S.E., Grand Rapids, Michigan 49506

Copyright © 1985 by Carol Kuykendall

Library of Congress Cataloging in Publication Data

Kuykendall, Carol, 1933-
    Learning to let go.

    "Pyranee books."
    Bibliography: p.
    1. Family—Religious life. 2. Parent and child. 3. Separation (Psychology) I. Title.
BV4526.2.K88   1985   248.8'4   85-17993
ISBN 0-310-33621-X

All Scripture quotations, unless otherwise noted, are taken from the HOLY BIBLE: NEW INTERNATIONAL VERSION (North American Edition). Copyright © 1973, 1978, 1984 by the International Bible Society. Used by permission of Zondervan Bible Publishers.

Edited by Lisa Garvelink
Designed by Ann Cherryman

Printed in the United States of America

86 87 88 89 90 / 10 9 8 7 6 5

Contents

Introduction

This is a personal book. I'm not a doctor or a counselor. I don't work with monkeys and mice, or with statistics and scientific data. And I'm not an expert.

I am a parent and a writer. And I'm interested in this subject because I have spent a lifetime bonding to my family: first to my parents, then to my husband and our three children.

Bonding comes easily to me. In fact, I can bond to a pet hamster within a few hours. It's cutting the bonds that bothers me, especially with our children. The letting-go process gets all mixed up with the holding-on instincts.

Learning to let go means releasing our children and allowing them to become people who don't need us anymore. It is, I've decided, one of the greatest challenges parents face.

Christian parents seem to have difficulty because we take our parenting responsibilities so seriously and care so deeply about the kind of people our children become. Even parents of grown children refuse to release the reins and recognize that their parenting responsibilities are over.

As a mother, I wrestle with this challenge. It is a struggle born of good intentions and deep emotions. I love our children intensely; I want to protect them instinctively; and I don't always recognize the ways I am holding on when I should be letting go.

Is he old enough to cross the street alone or ride a bike to school? Is she capable of buying her own clothes or determining her own curfew? When do I give up my control and trust the Lord to take over?

I was motivated to research this subject when I realized other parents were asking the same questions. "I read lots of books on how to be a good parent," a friend told me, "but none on how or when to give up that role."

I began gathering information from mothers, fathers, Christians, non-Christians, counselors, child psychologists, teachers, authors, and ministers. And I began formulating some key questions:

What does letting go mean?
How does it feel?
Why is it difficult?
Why must we do it?
What does the Bible say?
How do we do it? And when?

As a result of all my research, I found the best answers were neither clinical nor intellectual. Rather the answers came from parents like me who live with the problem and recognize that letting go is more than a physical act. It is a complicated emotional challenge that tugs at the very foundations of our family ties.

The purpose of this book is to combine all this information into a meaningful structure that might help other parents. This knowledge may not make letting go easier. But it may help us to do better parenting as we recognize the importance of our responsibility to love our children—and to let them go.

CHAPTER 1

Stirring Up the Nest

One bright spring day, our daughter Lindsay went off for her first sleepover at a friend's house. She excitedly packed her bag, kissed me goodbye, and skipped down the front steps. What bothered me most as she disappeared around the corner was that she didn't even look back.

As I turned and closed the door, I felt a familiar twinge of regret. It's one I've felt before, and I know I'll often feel again as I watch our children grow up and away from us. It is part of the process of letting go.

Letting go is a God-given responsibility, as important as love in the parent-child relationship. Without it, children cannot grow. With it, they gain the confidence and independence to seek and reach their potential in life.

"Give your children roots and wings," goes the old saying. Love them, protect them, and nurture them with a strong sense of God and family—and let them go.

Why is letting go difficult? Why do we get so tangled up in the apron strings? Why don't we push them out of the nest as easily as birds do? Why do we hold on when we should let go?

As the mother of three children in various stages of growing and going, I've wrestled with these questions for years and discovered several answers.

First, letting go contradicts our instincts. We love our

children. We want to protect them, fight their battles with them, and shield them from life's hurts. We want to nurture them close, not nudge them away.

Secondly, it is painful. Few human emotions are as intense as our love for our children. The birth of a child is one of the most dramatic events of a lifetime. The bonding in the moments, days, months, and years afterward is deeply significant in tying parents to children. No wonder, then, the slow severing of those bonds is a painful process that we resist.

Finally, letting go is bewildering. We feel ambivalent. Sometimes when the noise level is high and the satisfaction level is low, we long for the anticipated peace and quiet of the childless season of life. Yet, there are times when the children are all tucked into bed, smelling good and looking cherubic, that we can't imagine life without them.

Letting go presents us with a confusing conflict of parenting. It is a conflict of head and heart. Intellectually, we know our goals. We want our children to become confidently independent. Why, then, do we sometimes discourage rather than encourage their attempts? We raise our children to leave us. Why, then, does it hurt when they go?

These questions, even without answers, tell us one thing: Letting go is a complicated, continuing challenge for parents. It is not a single event that happens the day a child leaves home for college, an apartment, marriage, or a job. Rather it is a slow, physical and emotional process that starts the moment the umbilical cord is cut at birth and continues in little bits and pieces, moment by moment, as a child grows up. It is, in fact, a process with specific goals, characteristics, and a logical, predictable order of events. The goals of the letting-go process are twofold. They aim to prepare the child slowly for independence from the parents and to prepare the parents for life without the child.

The process has several spiritual goals. We raise our children to serve God—not us. We want them to become dependent on their heavenly Father—not us. We want them to learn that He will always be there—we won't.

The letting-go process demands a gradual change in the

way parents treat children. For instance, in the beginning we totally control the lives of our infant children.

In this infant stage, we show our love by protecting them. As they mature, however, we must change the way in which we show our love to them. Slowly and gently we must give up this protection and control and allow them to protect and control themselves.

We could think of this shifting balance mathematically. In the beginning, we have 100 percent control of their lives. By the time they leave home, they must have 100 percent control. In between, we transfer that control in a logical, orderly process. Slowly we let go, encouraging their independence. This logical transfer of control smooths the transitions we face in our changing relationships with our growing children. But there is no guarantee that the process will be smooth.

Actually, for me, letting go is difficult because I am an instinctive nest-maker. I love each of our three children and would do anything for them. Unfortunately, I sometimes do too much for them and smother them in the name of love instead of urging them to test their wings.

I hold on when I should let go because their going hurts, especially when I see some subtle little sign that reminds me they are growing up and away: the day I realized I had permanently become "Mom" instead of "Mommy"; or the time I discovered a "DO NOT DISTURB" sign on the door of the bedroom where I'd always been welcome; or the first time my child refused his usual goodbye kiss because his friends might see.

More subtle signs are in our future, and already I dread the first family vacation without the child who chooses to stay home; the first Thanksgiving with an empty place at the table; and the disappearance of the "DO NOT DISTURB" signs on bedroom doors because the occupants are gone. All these are perfectly predictable even desirable steps toward independence, but they are painful because each one cuts one more precious fiber in the tie that binds us.

Our challenge as parents is to view these steps of independence with pride instead of regret, while remembering that God has a purpose in this process. He often reminds us of that purpose by tucking little insights into our everyday experiences as He did for me one day last fall.

It started out as a seemingly typical struggle with learning to let go but ended up giving me an understanding of the letting-go process and has helped me cope ever since. The day dawned cool and clear, an early September morning. It was the first day of school in our neighborhood and an exciting day at our house. Kendall, our youngest, had finally reached the magic age of five, which gave her the right to buckle her shiny new shoes and to march out the door to kindergarten. She was ecstatic while I was torn between that familiar twinge of joy and regret.

I thought I had been looking forward to this milestone just as she was. After all, I had been home with little children for the last eleven years. In spite of periodic temptations to give up full-time mothering to seek the imagined fulfillment of a career, I chose to stay home and arrange my days around peanut-butter-and-jelly sandwiches, naptime schedules, and hectic preschool carpools.

Symbolically, that September day marked the beginning of the freedom and solitude I'd anticipated for years. Instead of excitement, however, I felt sadness. Even as I poured the breakfast cereal and brushed her tangled curls into ponytails, I realized this day also marked the end of the full-time mothering era of my life. Parenting is only a temporary job description, and I was about to take on a new part-time status that reminded me my parenting role had planned obsolescence.

I tried to swallow my nostalgia and share Kendall's joy when I walked her down the driveway. As the big yellow bus lumbered to a stop at our gate, I hugged her tightly and then let her go.

Tears stung my eyes as I watched the bus swallow her up and take her away. Angry at myself for feeling sad, I turned to walk back to the house. *Why should this normal, anticipated event cause depression?* I asked myself, walking up the front steps.

Inside, I poured myself a cup of coffee and wandered

aimlessly around a strangely quiet and empty house. I sank down in a chair by the window and blew a ripple over the black surface of the coffee. Suddenly I noticed a beautiful large bird, gracefully soaring over the field outside. Tawny with distinctive white markings, it had a powerful, wide wingspan.

Again I remembered the image of birds pushing their young out of the nest. *They have the right idea,* I told myself. Instinctively and unemotionally, they simply push their young out of the nest without regret, as if they know nothing about empty-nest syndromes. Unfortunately, I do.

For as long as I can remember, I've heard frightening descriptions of the loneliness and depression parents feel when the last of their litter walks out the door and suddenly leaves the home quiet—and empty. Just a few days before, a friend had stopped by after sending the last of her five children to college. "It's awful," she admitted, trying to laugh in spite of the quiver in her voice. "After twenty-six years of having kids around, suddenly the house is too big and lonely. We can't remember where the years went so quickly."

The quiet house around me at that moment was a preview of my own empty nest. As I pondered these thoughts, I continued to watch the large bird in the bright blue sky. I was so captivated by the circling and soaring that for a long while I didn't even notice the smaller bird with identical markings, now darting in quick, jerky movements around the larger bird.

Obviously, I decided, this was a baby bird, testing its wings. Following, leaving, returning, circling, and trying to mimic the example of the graceful, strong, and confident larger bird.

For these two birds this was nothing more than a normal training session. For me it was a revelation. This changed my trite image of mother birds. They don't simply push their young out ·of the nest, I realized. Instead they spend time patiently training and preparing their young so they will be capable of leaving the nest.

And what about the act of pushing them out of the nest? In the Bible, Moses describes how eagles train their eaglets to fly. "Like an eagle that stirs up its nest and hovers over its young, that spreads its wings to catch them and carries them on its pinions" (Deut. 32:11).

The eagle stirs up its nest because it cares. The eagle cares enough to encourage the eaglet to test its wings and even forces it out of the nest, because what good is an eagle that can't fly? The parent eagle stirs up its nest because of love for the eaglet.

Yet the same parent eagle stands by during those test flights, fluttering over the young, spreading out its wings, catching them when they fall, patiently correcting, teaching, and inspiring them to try again. Finally, when the eaglet is capable, it flies away: strong and free and alone, ready and able to seek its potential in life because of the training it received.

I focused again on the two birds outside the window. Leaving me with an exhilarating awareness of God's presence, they circled and disappeared out of sight. I knew their appearance was more than a coincidence. As a Christian, I don't believe in coincidences anymore. Instead I believe God uses the timing of sights or thoughts to remind us gently of His presence and His promises. It might be the words of a song or childhood Sunday school lesson that come to mind when needed, the appropriateness of a sermon message or Scripture reading, the timing of an opportunity, or the appearance of a friend at just the right moment. For me the sight of those two birds proved inspirational in my moment of need. They assured me that God has a plan for my life and a purpose in the challenge I faced that day.

His plan includes the challenge of raising children. But that is only one of many challenges He has in store for me in a lifetime. He has loaned these children temporarily to my husband and me to love, nurture, train, and finally release so they may seek God's will for their lives apart from us. That is His purpose.

Squeezing every ounce of joy, love, and training out of our precious years together, we have a responsibility to do the very best we can with these children. We also have a responsibility to stir up the nest, allowing and encouraging our children to test their wings at the appropriate moments like today. We do this not because it's easy but because it's part of the plan for their lives and ours. Unless they go, they can't reach their potential in life. Unless they go, we can't see what else God has in mind for our lives.

Those thoughts, those birds, and those moments alone helped me through a difficult step in the letting-go process. There have been other difficult steps since then. I'm sure there will be more in my future.

God didn't promise His challenges would be easy, including the challenge of raising children. But nothing worthwhile is ever accomplished without a measure of sacrifice or sorrow. And we know that suffering brings growth, and growth brings reward. Beyond the depression about Kendall's going off to school was a new burst of energy to tackle projects I'd never had time for previously.

There was another reward buried in that experience. When Kendall climbed on that bus with enthusiasm and confidence, she didn't look back. She cut a thread in the cord that binds us, and naturally I felt a twinge of regret. But her attitude told me I was succeeding in the challenge God had given me.

As our children conquer each milestone of independence, they tell us we are doing our job. What better reward do we need? Give your children roots and wings. I've written this saying on a card and taped it above my desk where I see it every day.

Roots go deep and help our children grow strong. They ground them against the assaults of the world and stabilize them. Roots come from bonding, loving, communicating, making memories, and observing traditions.

Wings lift children upward and inspire them. They help them soar freely, strongly, and close to God. They come from letting go, cutting ties, pushing off, and stirring up the nest. Children need both. Roots I can handle; wings are my challenge.

CHAPTER 2

Holding Things Loosely: The Letting-Go Process

"Your mother thinks she's having a heart attack," the voice on the phone said early one August morning last summer.

We lived next door. So I raced across the field on the well-worn path, into the house, and to her bedside. I held her hand and tried to talk her out of dying.

"It's okay, Mother. Relax, and breathe gently," I pleaded.

She shook her head slightly.

"This is the way I wanted it," she whispered, referring to her wish to die quickly. For years she had suffered from emphysema and she feared a slow, suffocating death.

A few minutes later it was all over, and my sixty-seven-year-old mother was gone. For weeks afterward, the painful memory of holding her hand and watching her die haunted me. In time I had to make a conscious and prayerful effort to let go of that powerful memory so I could recall the joy of her living and appreciate the victory she achieved in dying.

Letting go is a broad concept, a key to coping with life's everyday challenges. Generally it means giving up something—a self-centered emotion, an instinctive reaction or desire to control, even a material possession—to achieve a long-range goal for a greater good.

A woman lets go of her rigid, self-determined expectations of marriage to live with and love her husband and to save their marriage. A mother lets go of her fanatical desire for a spotless house to allow her children to make cookies, have friends over, or experiment with projects for the science fair. A dad, the neighborhood soccer coach, has to let go of his desire to win the big game (which he could win with his star players) to rotate all the players in and out of the lineup fairly.

The challenge in letting go is the act of putting aside or rising above our feelings. That is difficult because feelings are powerful. We cling to them, wallow in them, and allow them to control us.

We live in an age where we are encouraged to respect and respond to our feelings. We are told to "let it all hang out," "tell it like it is," or "if it feels good, do it." We also are told to be true to ourselves and share our feelings with others, regardless of the impact: Honesty at all costs.

No wonder Christians need to learn how to let go to live a godly life. But God equips us for the challenge. We have the wisdom of his Word, the communication with Him through prayer, and the enabling power of the Holy Spirit.

The Word helps us recognize our worldly, self-centered actions or responses and identify the godly response we should be seeking. Through prayer we receive the power of the Holy Spirit that enables us to let go of the human response and substitute the godly response. God works through us in this process.

We let go of our resentment and allow forgiveness. We let go of our anger and develop patience. We let go of our fears about tomorrow to appreciate the joys of today. Letting go becomes the tool that allows us to live our faith.

In other words, the Christian concept of letting go is a process that demands God's participation. It means knowing and claiming God's promises and being fully persuaded that God has power to do what He promises. It means giving up how we feel, what we think, or what we desire and choosing instead to yield ourselves to God.

When God told the faithful Abraham that He would give him a son, Abraham believed God in spite of the seeming

absurdity of the promise. After all, Abraham was one
hundred years old, and his wife Sarah was ninety.

> *Without weakening in his faith, he faced the fact that his body was*
> *as good as dead—since he was about a hundred years old—and*
> *that Sarah's womb was also dead. Yet he did not waver through*
> *unbelief regarding the promise of God, but was strengthened in his*
> *faith and gave glory to God, being fully persuaded that God had*
> *power to do what he had promised (Romans 4:19–21).*

Abraham was rewarded for his faith with a son, Isaac.

For us, just as for Abraham, letting go is a process of
aligning our will with His will in spite of our doubting
thoughts. Life is a series of challenges in letting go, and
growth in the Christian faith comes from succeeding in this
process.

As Christians, we let go of our children in the same
manner. The process demands God's participation. Through
faith in prayer, we claim God's promises and act on them.
Obediently we surrender our children to God as Abraham
obediently surrendered his only and beloved son Isaac to
God.

Imagine Abraham's feelings when he heard God command him to go to Mt. Moriah and sacrifice his son as a
burnt offering. How could obedient Abraham argue with the
Lord? He knew this son Isaac was truly a gift from God and
not his possession. Again because of his faith, Abraham
saddled his donkey, took his son, a knife, and the wood to
start the fire, and traveled three days to Mt. Moriah. He built
an altar, arranged the wood, bound his son, and laid him on
the altar. Just as he was ready to plunge the knife into his son,
the Lord stopped him and said: "because you have done this,
and have not withheld your son, your only son, I will indeed
bless you" (Gen. 22:16–17 RSV).

This Scripture teaches us about the letting-go process.
Whatever we hold on to—whether it be our material
possessions, our desires and feelings, or our children—the
Lord will ask us to release. What we willingly release to the
Lord, He will replace with something better. He rewards our

obedience. "I tell you the truth, whatever you bind on earth will be bound in heaven, and whatever you loose on earth will be loosed in heaven" (Matt. 18:18). As parents, we must daily walk to Mt. Moriah as Abraham did with an attitude of total surrender.

LETTING GO AS A PROCESS

Letting go—releasing our children—is a gradual process with distinguishing characteristics, predictable steps, and identifiable goals. It demands a sensitive balance of holding on and pushing off as Christian psychiatrist John White explains:

> *To relinquish your children does not mean to abandon them, however, but to give them back to God and in so doing, to take your own hands off them. It means neither to neglect your responsibilities towards them nor to relinquish the authority you need to fulfill those responsibilities. It means to release those controls that arise from needless fears or selfish ambitions.*[1]

We can control our children too tightly, overprotecting and stifling them. Or we can abandon them, allowing them to make choices and assume responsibilities they are not yet prepared to handle. The letting-go process is the slow, orderly transfer of freedom and responsibility from parent to child, from the moment of birth to maturity. It is a cognitive building process in which children gain self-confidence as they gain independence.

Although many privileges and responsibilities are considered age-appropriate, the letting-go process is more dependent upon the logical transfer of these responsibilities than their suggested age-appropriateness. The child gains freedom as he or she demonstrates ability to cope with responsibilities. A child builds upon past experiences, and ideally the responsibilities increase in number and importance each year.

How does a child demonstrate the ability to cope with responsibilities? Dependability seems to be important. If the child demonstrates predictable behavior in a given situation, the parent begins to trust him or her with that responsibility.

For instance, I let our children cross the street alone when I thought (and prayed) that I could count on them to look both ways, wait for approaching cars to pass, and use good judgment in deciding when to scurry across. When they became predictable in using this pattern of habits, I gave them the responsibility and privilege of crossing the street alone.

I began to leave them home alone for short periods of time when they exercised good judgment predictably and their unsupervised behavior was predictably good. I felt safe in assuming they wouldn't burn the house down, hurt each other, or disrupt the neighborhood. They knew how to dial 911 and handle an emergency.

If, however, I returned home one day and found broken furniture, black eyes, and goldfish on the floor, they would lose the privilege of staying home alone until they again became dependable.

When they handled short periods of time alone sufficiently well, I increased the amount of time. I built upon their successes and rewarded their capabilities.

In the letting-go process, we build upon a firm foundation of values and structure established early in life and enforced by strict discipline and control. As they grow, we loosen, not tighten, the reins. If we reverse this order and are permissive when they are young and then tighten our control as they grow and seek independence, we are in for a tough time. So are they. For instance, parents who rarely demand obedience and inconsistently enforce the rules with their preschoolers will have a hard time when they insist their sixteen-year-old be home by midnight. We cannot be stricter when they are older than when they were young.

It's like the theory that you can't teach an old dog new tricks. I know the truth of that proverb from experience. We have a spirited, independent, lovable young dog named Dutchess. Our children scooped her out of a litter of puppies at the Humane Society, brought her home, and allowed her adorable puppy traits to become bad habits. Curled into a cute little ball of fur, she slept on their beds. Now as a big dog, she can't distinguish between their beds and the living room couch, and she's too big for either spot. Try as we may, we can't take away a privilege she had as a puppy.

GENERAL RULES OF LETTING GO

The letting-go process, then, has some general rules:

1. Loosen, don't tighten, the controls as children grow.

2. Encourage and reward, instead of discouraging, their growing independence by increasing their responsibilities and privileges year by year. The more we encourage and allow their independence, the less they will have to prove it by rebelling.

3. Teach them how to think, not what to think. Allow them to make decisions and to fail. Encourage them to become problem solvers.

4. Don't regularly do anything for them that they are capable of doing for themselves.

5. Recognize and nurture their individuality. They are unique personalities, not our clones. They are gifts, not possessions. We raise them to serve God, not us.

6. Keep our goals in mind. Like a mountain climber striving to reach the summit, we must keep our eyes focused on our goals and not on the thorny bushes and slippery rocks that discourage and impede our progress along the way. We raise our children to leave us. Our responsibility is to equip and to prepare them for life without us. Their success is our success.

CHAPTER 3

Why Letting Go Is Difficult

A college friend, now a young husband, shocked me one day when he announced, "I don't think we'll have children. It's not worth it. I mean you invest all that time and emotion, and in a few years, they leave you. I don't think I could take it."

I was at a loss to respond. How do you explain to someone that having children is worth it in spite of the nights of interrupted sleep, the runny noses, spilled orange juice, sibling rivalry, and moody silences? All that and much more in exchange for sticky kisses, a refrigerator door covered with smudgy pictures of pointy suns and uneven rainbows, and a Mother's Day card that says, "You are the best mom in the whole world. You help me when I am in trouble."

How do I tell him that investing love in a child has inconsistent but unparalleled returns that grow in value in spite of the unwritten rule that the stock doesn't really belong to you? How do I tell him especially since he's a childless husband with an uncomplicated life, who has read the now-famous Ann Landers column that stated some 70 percent of the parents responding to a survey wouldn't even have kids if they could start over again.

I decide to tell him a silly story about our first dog because he understands about animals. Rhody was her name, a golden retriever from Rhode Island, and she was our first "child" as newlyweds. I raised her from a pup—newspaper training, obedience classes, the whole routine. She was a good dog, but she had her faults. She loved to roam, and I spent endless hours searching the neighborhood for her, always it seemed, just when I had to be somewhere else. She made me furious.

She cost us a lot not only in vet bills and kennel charges but in rental payments. Apartments would have been fine for us, but we always sought small houses in the country with yards so Rhody would be happy. We sacrificed for her too. We gave up spur-of-the-moment trips or dinner after work sometimes because we had to get home to let the dog in or out.

But I bonded to that dog for thirteen years and when we buried her in the field behind our house, I cried and grieved our loss. She had enriched our days, widened our circle of love, and taught us some lessons in life. I miss her romping around the house, and I'm grateful she was part of our family.

I'm not sure my friend understood, but today, two years later, he's a daddy. He'll learn too that letting go is not easy. It seems unfair that pain is the price we pay for caring. In fact, the parents who spend the most time parenting have the hardest time letting go. The mothers who stay home with their children have a harder time adjusting to life without them. The parents who organize their lives around the children who need them seem to have more difficulty reorganizing their lives when children leave.

It doesn't seem fair, but God rejects the notion of fairness in the worldly sense. We don't get out of something just what we put into it. We don't seek tit for tat. We give without thought of return. And we try to make sense out of our emotions or responses with God's help.

I had a teacher once who continually told us that the more we understood a problem, the better equipped we were to handle it; the more knowledge we accumulated, the better we could cope. With that motivation, let's examine some reasons letting go is difficult.

Letting go is difficult because we love our children instinctively, intensely, and possessively.

Recently I read a newspaper account about the death of a twenty-six-year-old man who drowned while trying to save his six-year-old son. The two were in a kayak when the craft flipped over in a deep pond. The father managed to grab hold of his son and keep the boy's head above water while he pushed the youngster toward shore and into the outstretched arms of frantic bystanders. Exhausted, the father slipped below the surface and out of sight. His body was found about thirty minutes later, and he was pronounced dead.

He had given his life for the life of his son instinctively. This story is poignantly dramatic but not unique. As parents, many of us would give our lives for our children. It's the nature of the intense, protective love we feel instinctively for our children.

It is a love that almost defies word descriptions and must be experienced to be understood. Usually from the moment of conception, certainly from the first glimpse and touch, parents begin bonding to children. We build dreams for them. We weave our lives around theirs. Together, we make up a unit we call family. No wonder, then, we feel fragmented and uncomfortable as we unravel the ties that bind us.

WE VIEW THEM AS POSSESSIONS

Although we often view our children as possessions, they are not. The Bible is clear on this point: "Children are a gift from God. They are his reward" (Ps. 127:3 LB). What a precious gift!

As with all of God's gifts, we don't own our children. Even Kahlil Gibran wrote in *The Prophet*, "Your children are not your children. They are sons and daughters of Life's longing for itself. They come through you but not from you, and though they are with you yet they belong not to you."[1]

Being Christians, we know that we don't own anything in the self-centered sense of ownership. What we have—our talents, our money, our material possessions, and our children—all are gifts from God to be used for His glory and according to His purpose.

It is the feeling of possession that causes us trouble when releasing our children. Hannah, the mother described in

1 Samuel, was grieved because she was childless. "The Lord had closed her womb" (1 Sam. 1:6), we are told. Hannah was married to Elkanah, who also had another wife Peninnah. Peninnah had children, and she would provoke Hannah to irritate her because she was barren. Imagine the heartache!

Hannah prayed to the Lord to give her a son and vowed, "I will give him to the Lord all the days of his life" (1 Sam. 1:11). The Lord answered her prayer, and she had a son, Samuel. Hannah kept her promise to the Lord and cared for this precious gift of a child until he was weaned, probably at about age three.

Then she took him to live with Eli the priest and said, "I prayed for this child, and the Lord has granted me what I asked of Him. So now I give him to the Lord. For his whole life he will be given over to the Lord" (1 Sam. 1:27–28).

On many days of my life, I would have gladly surrendered a three-year-old to any willing taker; but that's not the message in this Scripture. Hannah dearly loved Samuel and didn't want to give him up. But she knew she didn't own him. She knew the child belonged to God, and she surrendered him at an early age to fulfill the Lord's purpose for his life. The more we possess something, whether an object or a person, the more pain we feel in letting go. We must hold on to everything, even our children, loosely.

WE NEED THEM

Somewhere along the way, our love, combined with our possessiveness, may result in the development of an abnormal need for our children. The dependency role unwittingly gets reversed, and we find ourselves dependent upon our children to fulfill a specific need in our lives.

It may be to hold a disintegrating marriage together. I once asked a friend whose marriage appeared headed for trouble, "Are your children more important to you than your husband?"

"Why, yes," she answered without hesitation, assuming that would be every mother's answer. Eventually, through counseling she realized she was getting more emotional satisfaction from her children than from her husband and she was establishing a dangerous pattern of dependence upon them.

Our children may be more demanding than our spouse, but if they become more important, we are headed for trouble. By definition, parenting is a temporary job description. Our children will come and go. Hopefully, our spouse will stay.

In response to a crisis or tragedy, we can become overly dependent on our children. A beautiful young mother told me that after her mother's death in a car accident several years ago, she took her daughter out of preschool to spend the days at home with her. "My reaction to the loss of my mother was to hold on tighter to my daughter," she admitted.

Contrast that story with the late Catherine Marshall's description of the adjustment she and her nine-year-old son faced after the sudden death of her husband Peter Marshall:

> *The highest function of my mother love would be fulfilled when my love was strong enough to cut the apron strings and let my adult child move off into his own life. I would succeed as a mother only when I had so reared my child that he would no longer have need of me. Yet this is not tragedy; it is growth. This is no betrayal of love. This is love.*[2]

Understandably, a single parent may become emotionally dependent upon a child as a companion or confidant to fill the void left by the spouse, or as a helper to do the chores a spouse would normally do. On the other hand, the child in a single-parent household may gain confidence and independence from the responsibilities he or she shoulders out of necessity.

Many parents live through their children and see them as clones of themselves or encourage them to become what they are not. A father may push his son to become the athlete he was or wishes he had been. A mother may push her daughter to achieve what she didn't. David Elkind, in his book *The Hurried Child*, ventures that there is a strong connection between a parent's job dissatisfaction and a disproportionate concern with the offspring's success in sports.[3]

Whatever the reasons, parents seem to get emotionally involved in their children's athletic events. I call it "the Little League syndrome," a time when normally calm, rational parents as they "get into the game" shout or scream at referees, coaches, and even their own children

In our community, such behavior prompted the soccer league to establish a "Parents' Code of Conduct" that states:

> *Children have more need of example than criticism: Attempt to relieve the pressure of competition, not increase it; do not openly question an official's judgment and honesty. Officials are symbols of fair play, integrity and sportsmanship: Accept the results of each game by encouraging your child to be gracious in victory and to turn defeat into victory by working toward improvement.*

Sometimes we become dependent on our children because our identity is wrapped up in them. They are our total reason for being. Especially women seem vulnerable to this. Our children's dependence on us becomes our excuse not to do or be anything else. We use them to rationalize our full-time-mother status.

Obviously, there is a period in life when children are a legitimate excuse not to do anything else. I distinctly remember how I felt after the birth of each of our children. It was as if the world had stopped to allow me to be this baby's mother. No one expected me to do laundry, shopping, or cooking. Momentarily, my purpose in life was clearly defined: I was to nurture this baby.

That singleness of purpose didn't last long. In fact if I suffered a post-partum depression, it was because I realized we were two separate individuals, no longer symbiotic, and I had to pick up the plow and head on down the field to tend to my other responsibilities.

Yet a woman with babies and toddlers at home still has a legitimate reason not to do much else. There is little time or energy. That's why the first day of school for the youngest child can be a traumatic moment for the mother who has stayed home to care for her family. While the child may fear the unknown world of kindergarten, the mother fears the redefinition of her purpose in life.

Erma Bombeck, in *Motherhood, The Second Oldest Profession*, describes a mother's feelings as she watches the last of her litter march off to school:

> *My excuse for everything just got on that bus. My excuse for not dieting, not getting a full-time job, not cleaning house, not re-upholstering the furniture, not going back to school, not having order in my life, not cleaning the oven.*
>
> *It is the end of an era. Now what do I do for the next 20 years of my life.*[4]

Some women put off that moment of decision and simply have another excuse. These excuses are called "boredom babies." The rationale is simple: It's easier to have another baby than to decide how to get on with life.

I know someone like that. She has a twelve-year-old, a six-year-old, and a baby. I saw her recently, pushing a stroller. "I'm so wrapped up in this baby," she gushed, sweeping him up in her arms and covering his cheeks with kisses. I was glad for her, yet also a bit sorry because I knew that inevitably she would have to face the reality of life without a baby.

WE FEAR THEIR GROWING UP AND AWAY FROM US

Just as my college friend expressed, parents fear the pain of physical and emotional separation from their children. Is this separation more difficult for some than for others? Is it different for a mother, father, single parent, or Christian parent? As one counselor explained, what controls the level of difficulty is not so much the status as the emotional make-up of the person and the established pattern of the relationship.

Mothers and fathers may face the release of sons and daughters differently because of the subtle ways we treat them differently as they grow up. Some mothers tend to overprotect sons and consequently have a harder time handing them over to future daughters-in-law. But these same mothers may expect more out of their daughters as they grow up. "Up until we left home, my mother always asked my brother what he wanted for lunch and always expected me to fix my own lunch," one college student told me.

Fathers tend to overprotect their daughters and encourage their sons to be tough. Fathers usually face fewer life changes than mothers as their children mature. Generally, their going off to school doesn't disrupt a dad's schedule as much or tug at his emotions as obviously unless he is a single parent raising his children. And single parents often are forced to let go emotionally and physically when they share custody of their growing children.

Although mothers by nature are nest-makers, they sometimes are more prepared for the final release than fathers because they gradually adjust to a quiet nest along the way. Weaning, preschool, and finally all-day-long school give mothers a chance to let go slowly.

As stated previously, Christian parents often have difficulty letting go because we care so much about the kind of people our children become. We invest so much of ourselves and our values into their lives. We fear the temptations they face in the world beyond our doorsteps and the consequences of the actions they choose.

In his book, *Adolescent-Parental Separation*, clinical psychologist Michael Bloom describes parents who do and don't let go easily. Those who let go easily are self-confident, comfortable with change, good at interpersonal relationships, able to learn from their adolescents, and able to satisfy their own needs as well as their children's. They also value independence and autonomy for themselves and their children, have a clear sense of personal values, and see the separation process as a natural part of growth.

Parents who have difficulty letting go have a low sense of autonomy, are less clear about values and identity, are uneasy about communicating differences with others, and view the separation process as desertion by their children.[5]

Personally, I fear our children growing up and away from us. Emotionally, I resist the rejection and rebellion that are an inevitable part of the separation process. The ties cannot be cut without some tearing. And I've had previews already. "Please don't wear THAT skirt to field day, Mom." Or "Just wait in the car when you come pick me up." It used to be that I could burn the bacon, choose their clothes, even tell the barber how to cut their hair, without a comment from them. Now I can't even choose my own clothes without their criticism.

Physically, I fear the anticipated loneliness of our home without them. Like the mothers who have boredom babies, I used to dream of surrounding myself with a houseful of children as some sort of assurance that I would never be lonely. I like being a mother and I can't give up without some regret an era of my life that I've enjoyed.

The passing of this era not only makes me nostalgic but it also makes me face the reality of my own physical mortality. Just as the death of both my parents gave me a raw, unsettling awareness of a generation gone by, so the emptying of our nest will edge me a step closer to my own physical passing.

WE FEAR THE CONSEQUENCES OF OUR CHILDREN'S ACTIONS

We fear letting go and allowing them to make their own choices and decisions because what they do reflects on us. Children are our report cards for parenting. Whether it is because of our pride or possessiveness, we are afraid to let them fail. Their failures not only hurt them but we think they also reflect badly on us especially in front of our own parents, Aunt Tillie, or the nearly perfect parent down the street, who subtly compares her children with our children all the time. Author and mother Phyllis Theroux writes: "We hold our children up, like mirrors, and search the reflection for proof that we have not failed, ostensibly as parents, in reality as human beings. Hard on ourselves, we are often doubly hard on them, asking them to perform better than we can."[6]

LETTING GO IS A CONFUSING PROCESS

We feel ambivalent. One moment I long for the time when I can stay in bed all day long when I'm sick, read the newspaper without interruption, and have some privacy without locking myself in the bathroom. The next minute I am overwhelmed with the warm sense of family as all five of us ski down a mountainside together, and I want to reach out and stop the hands of time.

We feel confused with a mixture of pride and regret as we recognize their growing independence. One of our children came home from school obviously rankled about something. After downing a peanut butter sandwich and milk in silence, this was confessed: "Something happened today at school, but I don't want to tell you about it. It wasn't bad. It just hurt my feelings. It's okay though. I've already prayed about it."

Proud? Yes.

Curious? Certainly!

Feeling left out? You bet!

We're confused because letting go is also a process that demands a gradual change in the way we treat our children. We give them more responsibility and allow them more freedom as they grow up. The shift of control means we must change the way we show our love for them. We constantly redefine our relationship with them. Essentially, our goal is to change from a parent-child relationship to an adult-adult relationship and we make the transition smoother by letting go as they mature.

Author Michael Bloom describes this change as the "death of the child-parent relationship," a death that often causes both parent and child a period of bereavement in response to the loss. He explains that to make the transition, many needs previously fulfilled by the relationship must be withdrawn, and "certain expectations, modes of response, and fulfillments must die. The powerful child-parent relationship so necessary to child development must now die in order to allow the young adult to pursue independently his or her future."[7]

How does all this translate into behavior patterns within a family? I'll give you an example. Recently, a woman, who was attending a seminar I was teaching about the subject of "Letting Go," admitted to our group, "I'm frustrated and I need some answers. I get along just fine with my four-year-old but I simply can't cope with my fourteen-year-old. Why? After all, I'm the same mother."

Her question and frustration make a major point in the subject of letting go. We cannot be the same parent to a four-year-old that we are to our fourteen-year-old. Their ages demand that we treat them differently. We leave lots more slack in the string with a teenager than with a preschooler.

Letting go is confusing because it is a roller coaster for both parents and children. It is disconcerting to watch our little cherubs yo-yo in and out of the nest as they grow up. We go from being needed twenty-four hours a day to hardly getting a one word response from them.

The four-year-old who fiercely demands to choose her own clothes in the morning is shy and reluctant to enter the door of her preschool classroom. The preadolescent who cries in the morning because her bangs won't curl right is the same child who takes her teddy bear to bed that night. The thirteen-year-old who sulks at dinner because the upcoming family vacation sounds "boring" is the one who needs a longer-than-usual goodnight hug a few hours later.

And finally, letting go is confusing because it presents us with a conflict between head and heart. In our heads, we know our goals. We want to toughen, prepare, teach, and release our children. But sometimes our progress is thwarted by the instinctive, protective love in our hearts.

I'm reminded of the interview I had with a child psychologist who is also a mother. She knew all the answers. From cleaning their plates to carrying out the garbage, she knew how to make kids accept their responsibilities cheerfully and effectively. It sounded so simple. She sounded so perfect.

Finally, I put down my pencil, looked at her, and asked, "Do you really do all this at home? Does it work?"

"Of course I don't do it all," she quickly answered. "When they are your kids, your mother heart takes over for your head knowledge." Letting go is difficult because all too often our hearts win out over our heads.

CHAPTER 4

Why We Must Let Go

Through the years I've learned many things about myself. For one thing, I'm a procrastinator, who is not motivated to tackle a problem until I understand, sometimes dramatically, why a solution is necessary. Too often a problem has to reach the crisis stage before it catches my attention.

Take our washing machine, for instance. It doesn't automatically flip into the next cycle anymore. Once started, it just hums away in the wash cycle until I come to the rescue and manually flip it into the rinse cycle. It's a clumsy solution but it works, and I'm not motivated to call the repairman yet.

"Why live with a problem you can solve?" one of my more efficient, organized friends asked me one day.

"Why solve a problem you can live with?" I responded.

No wonder I had the same attitude about letting go of our children. Why worry about a problem when they are years away from leaving the nest? Besides, I knew the theories. And I could parrot God's promises: He loves them more than we do; He knows them better; and He has a plan for their lives that He ultimately controls—we don't.

Each morning for years, I claimed these promises in prayers. But as soon as I said, "Amen," I went right on trying to control their day-to-day activities and their futures as if I had no faith in the promises I claimed. I didn't really understand what it meant to let go of that control until our family came up against a crisis that shattered our security and threatened the life of one of our children.

WE LET GO BECAUSE WE DO NOT CONTROL THEIR LIVES

It was a day indelibly marked in my memory, Sunday morning, March 22, 1981. We thought our nine-year-old son had been coming down with the flu the night before because he kept throwing up. He spent a restless night snuggled in a puffy comforter on the floor by our bed, the privileged spot reserved for sick children in our family. He was in and out of the bathroom all night long and by dawn, he looked frighteningly pale and dehydrated. He kept whimpering for something to drink, but even sucking an ice cube triggered his retching again.

I hated to bother the doctor on a Sunday morning, but obviously this child needed some medicine to stop his vomiting. When I reached our pediatrician, he asked a few seemingly routine questions and told me to meet him at his office in half an hour. "And," he instructed, "bring along a urine sample." That was no problem. My son was going to the bathroom often.

My husband Lynn and the two girls went off to Sunday school, and I cheerfully told them we would be home before they were. We weren't.

When we got to the doctor's office, I helped my son out of the car. He seemed weak and suddenly thinner. The doctor met us at the door, put us in an examining room, and took the urine specimen down the hall to a lab room. I heard the clinking of instruments and then his approaching footsteps, which echoed eerily in the empty office. He joined us and looked down at my son who was crumpled in a heap on the examining table.

"We have diabetes here," he announced quietly. "He needs to go to the hospital immediately where they will start IV's to stabilize him." His next words grew muffled as the first numbing waves of shock swept over me, momentarily protecting me from the pain of comprehending.

"Diabetes . . . " as the word echoed through my head, strange, fearful, and unknown visions of frail, limp-wristed victims flashed through my mind. They had nothing to do with this normally athletic, energetic boy.

Within a few minutes we were our way out of the doctor's office. We had come in, thinking my son had the flu and expecting a prescription and some advice. Instead, we were rushing to the hospital with something incurable and potentially life-threatening. For the first time in our lives, there was no prescription; there was no cure.

The next several hours were a hazy blur of activities, but slowly the impact of the diagnosis began to sink in as the doctor and nurses answered our questions and explained juvenile diabetes.

For some reason our son's pancreas no longer produced sufficient insulin to meet his body's needs. He would have to take insulin injections every day to survive. He would also have to follow a strict diet and carefully balance his food intake with regular exercise. We would have to monitor his control with daily blood or urine tests and learn to detect and deal with the inevitable insulin reactions. In spite of these precautions, our son still might face the complications that threaten all diabetics, such as blindness, kidney failure, or heart problems. It was overwhelming.

Our little boy lay quietly on the bed as the doctor spoke. Although the IV solution was slowly giving him strength, he didn't yet comprehend the meaning of all this. Maybe, just for now, we could protect him from the painful realization that diabetes could rob him of his carefree childhood and endanger his future.

Later that night, Lynn and I sat holding hands beside our son's hospital bed. It had been an emotionally exhausting night, and we both ached as we looked at our sleeping child, anchored to his bed by the tubes running into his body. He looked so young and helpless.

Aware for the first time of our inability to control our son's future, we felt helpless too. Quietly we prayed together that night, releasing our child to the Lord. As well as I can remember, this was our prayer:

Lord, we've always had trouble believing that you love our children more than we do and that you will take care of them. We know we've tried to control their lives. But Lord for the first time, we face a problem with no human solution. We can't cure it or change it. So we come to you in humble dependence and place this child in your hands tonight. We know you have a plan for his life. Please take care of him and help us to accept that plan with loving support. . . .

Ever since that night, we've understood the total surrender of letting go. And we've been rewarded with the peace and strength needed to face the subsequent challenges of letting him go and allowing him to lead a normal life in spite of his diabetes. We clung to our faith as he went back to school, ran a six-mile race, and jetted off to another state for three days with his rope-jumping demonstration team.

"God isn't completely free to work in a child's life until we let go of that child and leave him or her entirely in God's hands," claims author Margie Lewis in a booklet "Hope for the Hurting Parent."[1] That's a powerful reason not to procrastinate.

A father told me how he's learned to let go in situations where he has no control. "We've faced a lot of crises in high school and college with our four kids. Drugs, school failures, serious weight problems, total lack of motivation," he related. "The pivotal point in each crisis was letting go. We told them we couldn't control their behavior, so the responsibility and therefore the consequences were theirs. We continued to offer support and advice, but we quit nagging. In each case, there was a dramatic change. They took control and solved the problems."

WE LET GO IN OBEDIENCE TO GOD

For Christian parents, it's important that the Bible tells us to let go. God has a clear plan for families: "A man will leave his father and mother and be united to his wife, and they will become one flesh" (Gen. 2:24).

We are told, however, to give up our childish ways much before marriage: "When I was a child, I talked like a child, I thought like a child, I reasoned like a child. When I became a man, I put childish ways behind me" (1 Cor. 13:11). Also, "we are to grow up in every way into Him who is the Head, into Christ" (Eph. 4:15 RSV).

Our children will not give up their childish ways unless they sever their bonds of dependency upon us. They cannot grow up in every way unless we withdraw our control from their lives to allow them to mature independently. So we teach them God desires "godly offspring" (Mal. 2:15), but we can't learn for them. It's the old "Don't touch the stove because it's hot" theory. We warn children, but they don't believe us until they touch the stove. Then they learn and they don't forget. We have to let go and give them the freedom to learn for themselves and to allow them to fulfill God's purpose for their lives—not ours.

Jesus himself is an example of a child growing up to fulfill God's purpose for his life. Imagine his mother Mary standing at the foot of the cross, witnessing the agonizing death of her son. The child she bore and held in her arms was being torn from her in death. What pain she must have felt! Yet, Jesus had to die on the cross to fulfill God's greater purpose for his life.

Mary had to face separation that day, but she had been learning to let go all through his life as she realized this was God's child more than her own. Imagine how she felt when she and Jesus' brothers came upon him speaking to a crowd. When informed that his mother and brothers were waiting for him, Jesus replied, "Who is my mother, and who are my brothers?" Pointing to his disciples, he said, "Here are my mother and my brothers. For whoever does the will of my Father in heaven is my brother and sister and mother" (Matt. 12:48–50).

She had to let go: She had to let Jesus meet the tests of faith so that he might learn the endurance that would prepare him for God's planned experience on the cross. The Bible tells us God has a plan for our children too. They are God's children, and we must let go to allow God to guide them toward the discovery of his plan for them.

WE LET GO BECAUSE WE LOVE THEM

Another reason we must let go is because we love our children. In the last chapter, we learned letting go is difficult because we love our children. This same love is the reason we must let go. Consider for a moment the hopes we have for our children. What do we want out of life for them? What qualities do we hope they possess when they leave home?

When these questions were posed to a Christian parenting group recently, they quickly came up with some answers.

— Personal relationship with Christ
— Spiritual growth
— Development of self-esteem and confidence
— Ability to withstand peer pressure
— Working knowledge of their gifts
— Appreciation of the family as valuable
— Ability to accept responsibility
— A rewarding career

If we look back over these goals, we realize the route reaching them is through our children's gradual release from us as parents. We want them to have a personal relationship with Christ, but they don't inherit that from us. They must choose that for themselves.

We hope they recognize their gifts and grow up to feel confident and capable in life, but their self-esteem comes partly from learning to pick themselves up after failing especially when we're not around to help. We have to give them the freedom to gain confidence in themselves apart from us.

"One of the highest priorities I have is to teach my children to live life without me," author Karen Burton Mains told a roomful of mothers at a women's conference. "I want them to learn to be dependent upon their heavenly Father who will always be with them—I won't."

WE LET GO FOR OUR OWN GOOD

Our children's growing independence is not only good for them, but it is good for us too. The child-rearing season of life has a certain set of expectations. We expect, for instance, to put forth a maximum amount of time and energy in their infancy and toddler years. We expect to get a bit of a break during their school years, not only because they are away from home more often, but because they do more for themselves and make more of their own decisions. If we do not allow this change to occur naturally, we are likely to get tired. I recently found the following quote in an inspirational booklet for mothers:

> *Being a mother is*
> *a lot like teaching a child*
> *to ride a bicycle.*
> *You have to know when*
> *to hold on and when to*
> *let go. If you lack this courage*
> *to let go, you'll get very tired of running along beside.*[2]

This kind of parental fatigue is also known as "parent burnout," and Joseph Procaccini, a national authority on family relationships, has written a book on the subject. He describes burnout as a physically, emotionally, and some-times spiritually exhausted reaction to the stress of raising children. He estimates burnout affects about half of the parents in the United States, including both fathers and mothers. According to Procaccini, parents especially vulnerable to burnout are those types

> *. . . who want to control their children from infancy to age 35.*
> *They have the script and they are the directors; children are to*
> *perform accordingly. This is in contrast to parents who are*
> *developers. They are people who provide the basic support for a*
> *child's growth and progress, but they are willing to change with*
> *the child.*[3]

WE MUST LET GO BECAUSE THE TIES THAT BIND CAN ALSO STRANGLE

Because we love our children, we can smother them with protection. It's easy to do because providing protection is a normal characteristic of a love relationship. So is overprotection.

One afternoon a couple of years ago, I visited my father-in-law in the hospital. He was recovering from minor surgery, but at age seventy-four the experience frightened him, and he shared with me his concern that he had not prepared my mother-in-law for life without him.

"I think I've done too much for her over the years," he said regretfully. "Driving her places, paying the bills, fixing everything. Now I'm worried she couldn't get along on her own."

When we love someone, we enjoy doing things for that person. But in a love relationship, we also have a responsibility not to allow our protective love to stifle the growth of others—especially our children. We have to realize that we can hurt them by doing too much.

Dr. James Dobson recognizes our instinctive, protective love but encourages parents to temper it:

> *We want to rise like a mighty shield to protect them from life's sting—to hold them snugly within the safety of our embrace. Yet there are times when we must let them struggle. Children can't grow without taking risks. Toddlers can't walk initially without falling down. Students can't learn without facing some hardships. And ultimately, an adolescent can't enter young adulthood until we release him from our protective custody.*[4]

What are some signs and consequences of overprotection? Inappropriately trying to control a child's environment is a sign of overprotection. Our children's preschool teacher has a name for overprotective mothers. She calls them "smother mothers." The smother mother is the one who lingers at school each morning, hanging up her child's coat, tying on the paint apron, helping to spread peanut butter on a cracker, and doing all the other things the child is capable of doing.

"Not only is this unhealthy for the mother," the teacher claims, "but it robs the child of the important sense of self-confidence he or she needs to be building at this stage of life."

My daughter has a friend whose mother always has an excuse why her nine-year-old can't go swimming with us, sleep over at our house, or go to a movie. She rarely goes anywhere without her parents. This same mother couldn't understand why her daughter was afraid to start school at the beginning of fourth grade.

The consequences of overprotecting by controlling our children's environment are contrary to our goals for them. We run the risk of raising emotionally handicapped children who are paralyzed with dependence upon their parents. They lack the confidence to try a new experience, make a decision, or face life alone. At age twenty-three, they may still be living at home trying to find themselves, while Mom and Dad are footing the bills, getting their meals, and doing the laundry.

But not all children react to overprotection with compliance. Some suddenly rebel to defy their parents and finally free themselves of their parents' stifling control. Child psychiatrist Foster Cline calls this "hostile dependency," a condition that brews during adolescence when a person unconsciously comes to believe that he needs protection but consciously resents every minute of it.[5] The more we learn about anorexia, bulimia, and other eating disorders the more we see these problems as forms of rebellion against parents' overprotectiveness.

Running away from home is another form of rebellion. A story in a recent national magazine described the disappearance of a sixteen-year-old girl, the only child of overly protective parents who insisted upon driving her to and from high school each day. The daughter who appeared compliant ran away to the streets of New York City with little money and no friends to free herself herself from her parents' smothering protection. More than two weeks later, she returned home to her parents who finally realized they had to give their daughter some independence and allow her to think for herself.[6]

A study of runaways and their relationships with their parents identifies three ways parents attempt to delay or prevent a child's separation, while actually triggering a child's decision to run away.

"Affective binding" is characterized by the parent overindulging the child with excessive rewards. "Giving, in this sense, has less to do with the real needs of the child than the parental drive to maintain strong, manipulative control over the child and thus prevent the child from becoming autonomous."

"Cognitive binding" happens when parents impose their perceptions and definitions upon their children to prevent them from acknowledging their own feelings. This results in low self-esteem and gets children into the habit of listening to voices outside their heads instead of inside their heads.

If children rely on instructions and direction from someone else instead of being taught to think for themselves, they are more susceptible to peer pressure and even cults and charismatic leaders as they grow up. They are vulnerable to being led by others stronger than themselves because they are accustomed to being told what to do.[8]

"Superego binding" is parents' excessive exploitation of their children's feelings of loyalties. Children are made to feel guilty at any thought of reducing their loyalties to their parents. All three types of parental behavior work toward the same intended goal: keeping the children unnaturally close to the parents.[7]

DON'T FIGHT THEIR BATTLES

We also control our children's environment and overprotect them by fighting their battles for them. We rush to their defense at school, in the neighborhood, and with friends, teachers, or coaches. Our desire to save them is instinctive and fierce.

I know because I've been there. I've often said that being a parent can bring out the worst in me. People can hurt me, but they don't dare mess with my kids. If someone hurts their feelings, I can turn into a mother bear. Almost involuntarily, I feel a snarl starting in the back of my throat. My lips curl back exposing my fangs, and my fingernails become claws ready to scratch my way through battle.

It happened just recently. We were spending a summer weekend at a large mountain cabin with two other families.

There were three girls about the same age including our ten-year-old daughter. From the moment we arrived, it was obvious the other two girls had established an exclusive friendship. It was two against one.

As the weekend progressed, I watched my daughter's hurt grow deeper. Occasionally she caught me alone and complained that they were being mean to her. Finally, the second afternoon she found me in our bedroom and fell in a heap on the bed beside me. "Mom, they're being so mean," she whimpered, putting her head on my shoulder and starting to cry.

That did it. I felt the snarl starting in the back of my throat. Listening to two little voices arguing inside me, I comforted her with my lips curling. One voice was saying, "Don't get involved. They will work it out." The other stronger one countered, "They have no right to be so rude. They should learn. . . ."

I listened to the second voice. After consoling my daughter, I marched out of the bedroom on my way to battle. I found the other two girls alone in the dining room, giggling and telling secrets. That fanned the final spark, and I ignited.

"I know it's really fun when you two get together," I said as nicely as I could, "but do you girls realize you have hurt someone else's feelings this weekend? Do you know how it feels to be left out?"

It was over quickly. They mumbled something, grabbed some potato chips, and left. But it wasn't over. Unfortunately, my daughter had overheard the conversation from the bedroom and she was horrified.

"Mom, how could you?" she wailed, when I returned to the bedroom. "You only made it worse. Now they'll think I'm a baby and you have to take care of me. I could have handled it, Mom!" And she could have.

Feeling calmer and more rational, I apologized. "You know," I told her, "there are times moms get so upset they do stupid things, like I just did, mostly because they love kids. Can you possibly understand?"

She nodded, reminding me of myself at her age when I decided to no longer confide all my hurts and fears to my mother because they always bothered her longer than they bothered me. My mother's overreactions cut off some of our communication.

I made a mistake that afternoon with my daughter. After all, it was a typical ten-year-old girl's problem. At that age, girls seem determined to form tight, cliquish circles as if they are oblivious to the feelings they hurt. Being on the outside helps one learn how painful exclusion can be.

My responsibility was to my daughter, not the other girls. I should have encouraged her but not gone to battle for her. She would have changed the circumstances without my interference or accepted the temporarily unpleasant situation. I continue to learn from experience that when I can't change a situation, at least I can change my attitude toward it. That's where I have power in a seemingly powerless situation. I have no right to shield my daughter from the opportunity of learning that same lesson.

LIFE ISN'T FAIR

There's another drawback to fighting our kids' battles for them. It teaches them to expect that life is always fair, or if it isn't, Mom or Dad will be there to make it fair.

I have a friend who is a high school counselor. She tells me about the parents who always fight their kids' battles, whether their kids are right or wrong; for instance, a girl can't cheerlead because her grades have slipped below the designated grade point average, or a boy is ineligible to suit up for the game Friday night because a certain teacher won't "give" him a higher grade on a test. Demanding that an exception be made for their son or daughter, these parents come storming to the teacher or counselor because this is an injustice—just like all the other injustices they've protected their children from throughout childhood.

Granted, there are times parents must come to the defense of their children. Some injustices can't and shouldn't be overlooked, and as parents we're challenged to make those difficult distinctions. The father of a high school student described the struggle he had with such a decision. "My daughter dropped from a straight 'A' to a 'B' in a favorite class, simply because we were on vacation and she missed a day of school. According to the teacher, missing class for any reason other than illness was an automatic grading penalty. I wrestled with the decision of whether I should talk to the teacher. It was an unfair, inflexible rule, but more importantly, I decided my daughter should learn that life is full of unfair rules I can't change."

I remember as a child, when faced with one of life's little injustices, I would wail to my parents, "But it isn't fair!" They would always answer with disgusting authority, "Life isn't fair, dear." They were right of course. Losing a parking place to a rude but quicker driver or giving up a planned trip because of a bad snowstorm are everyday examples that life isn't fair.

Our own children echo that same pitiful cry, and I'm always torn between wanting to make life fair for them and knowing I should toughen them up against all the inevitable unfairness they will face in the world. If we overprotect them from life's stings, we rob them of the opportunity to grow through suffering.

> *We rejoice in our sufferings, knowing that suffering produces endurance, and endurance produces character, and character produces hope, and hope does not disappoint us, because God's love has been poured into our hearts through the Holy Spirit which has been given to us (Rom. 5:3–5 RSV).*

Pain, more than joy, shapes our lives and motivates us to learn and grow. A searing burn teaches us not to touch the stove. When someone else hurts our feelings, we learn not to hurt others' feelings. Our children will not have the freedom to learn these lessons unless we let go of them. We let go in obedience to God because we cannot control their lives; most importantly, we let go because we love them.

CHAPTER 5

Children as Gifts—Not Possessions

When I was a child and asked my mother or father if I could do something, often they gave me a flat and final no for an answer.

"Why?" I would ask.

"Because I said so," they replied.

I remember a lot of those replies over the years, but the words never seemed to quite answer my questions. And the tone always bothered me though I didn't know exactly why.

Today as a mother, I think I understand better. There's a sense of authority and ownership about a reply like that. It doesn't really answer the question and doesn't grant the respect for the growing independence of a child.

Yet I must confess even with this insight, I sometimes find myself automatically and flatly saying no to our children in response to their requests.

"Can Ginny come over today?"

"No."

"Why?"

"Because I said so."

As soon as the words are out, I realize I don't mean that. I mean I am tired; I don't want to clean up the messes they might make, or even that I don't want to make that decision right now. But I say no because I want to end the subject instead of thinking it through or telling the child I need to wait an hour before deciding.

In a sense, the flat no answer comes from the way I see myself as a parent and the way I view that child in our home at that moment. I find myself slipping into the authoritative role of owner instead of viewing this child as an individual with different but legitimate desires.

Children are gifts from God, not possessions. They are human beings separate from us, not clones of us. And although they need our guidance, they deserve our respect.

"Do you treat your children as well as you treat your friends?" author Karen Burton Mains asked a group of women. "If not, why not? Aren't they more important?" Her question was blunt and revealing. If we don't treat our children at least as kindly as we treat our friends, we aren't giving them the respect they deserve. How do we talk to them? Do we exercise our authority without respect for their needs? Sometimes I do.

"Please set the table," I say to the child who is curled up on the couch, reading a book.

"Just a minute."

"No. Right now!" I demand.

"Mom! I want to finish this chapter."

The disagreement ends with my daughter slamming her book down and grudgingly setting the table. What if I put myself in the same situation? How do I feel when I'm reading and a child asks me to do something? Unless it's an emergency, I always say "Just a minute" and respond when I reach a stopping point in the book or magazine.

We didn't need the table set until dinner time, which was still thirty minutes away. My daughter knows it only takes her maybe four minutes to set the table. When she answered "Just a minute," I could have informed her calmly that we were eating in thirty minutes, so she needed to set it before then. I shouldn't interpret her stalling as a threat or challenge to my authority but as an honest expression of her legitimate desire at that moment.

BREEDING GUILT INTO THEM

We treat our children as possessions rather than gifts when we make them feel guilty about things. We communicate guilt not only through words but body language: a certain look, tone of voice, or facial expression. It's a manipulative move familiar to most parents, not only because we use it but because we remember the powerful guilt feelings of our childhood.

Many times, the guilt is motivated by the parent's need for appreciation. A friend told me her mother rarely bought her anything without using guilt to manipulate her appreciation. "I'm buying you this pair of shoes today because I'm not getting a coat," she often told her.

Here's another example. A mother makes a nice meal, but the children don't compliment her. So she begins to manipulate for their appreciation.

"So you didn't like the meal?" she asks with obvious sarcasm.

Stunned silence. "Well . . . sure, Mom," one offers.

"You didn't tell me you liked it," she responds, gathering momentum. "I slaved all afternoon just to try a new recipe and make a good meal, and what thanks do I get? None! Next time it will be TV dinners, that's for sure!"

When we manipulate our children through guilt, it's as if we believe they were put in our homes to please us. Their role is not to take care of our needs. Guilt is a powerful, overwhelming anxiety and can become a major problem in our communication with our children. Many parents continue to use guilt as a tool with their children long after childhood.

DISCOVER THEIR BENTS

If we view our children as gifts, separate from us and from each other, we are more able to recognize and encourage their individual bents, which is important to the development of their self-esteem and independence. Bents are not learned, automatically inherited, or shaped by the environment. Bents are God-given, inborn characteristics.

"He's a chip off the old block," or "She looks a lot like you" makes me secretly proud. But I must admit I'm even prouder when I see a six-year-old with chubby little hands, patiently finger-training her parakeet (when I have no such patience); an eight-year-old displaying the ability to ride a horse with grace and assurance (when her father and I are nonequestrian); and a ten-year-old with the self-discipline to give up sugar (when I lack such will power). I am in awe of their God-given gifts and their ability to mold me, even as I mold them.

Larry Christenson, in his book *The Christian Family,* writes:

> *Every person comes into the world, and comes into the Body of Christ, with "sealed orders"—a unique destiny to fulfill. Part of the calling of a parent is to help the child unseal his orders— discover what it is that God means him to be and do. We are to train up the child not simply in the way that any and every child should go, but also in* the *(specific and unique) way in which* he *should go.[1]*

As parents, we need to help our children discover what they do well. We need to train them in the way God made them to go, not the way we want them to go or the way the nosey neighbor thinks they should go. We need to train them up according to the individual gifts that God gave them.

How can parents recognize the bents in their children? It takes time, desire, and sensitivity. We have to get to know our kids by observing, listening, talking to, and spending time with them.

In his article, "Every Child Has a Gift," teacher and author Hughes Mearns states, "Though few children are geniuses, all children, I discovered, possess gifts which may become their special distinction." Based on fifty years of teaching, he advises parents to discover their children's unsuspected gifts through cool observation.

Observe them when they are off-guard, he suggests. Watch them at picnics, on the playground, during a game, or quietly at home. Observe them without judgment, as if they were someone else's children.

Stop trying to make them what they ought to be and see what they are now. Listen to them; encourage them to express their opinions at the dinner table or before bedtime. He concludes with this advice:

For some adults, discovering hidden gifts in children will demand a change in personality; for self-effacement in an adult is what draws the child out. Children think about the world and come to worthy conclusions—their own. They think about themselves and those around them and come to worthy conclusions—their own.[2]

When I registered our children in preschool, I had to fill out a detailed questionnaire for each. What is your child's favorite activity? What are his fears? What makes him sad? What makes him happy? What is his favorite color, book, and TV character? The questions made me feel uneasy because I didn't know the answers to all of them. But they also reminded me of my responsibility to get to know our kids.

It helps to share observations with teachers, coaches, friends, other parents, and especially spouses. It also helps to spend time whether planned or unplanned alone with each child. One father I know alternates which child he takes on out-of-town business trips, when his schedule permits. One mother makes a point taking turns with different children to do Saturday errands and have lunch together. I especially relish time alone in the car with a single child. For a few moments that child is my captive audience.

As children grow up, games can be a functional means of discerning differences, likes, and dislikes. One new game called the Ungame gets family members talking and learning about each other as they tell about favorites or play imaginary roles. A parent learns a daughter wants to live on a farm or a son dreams of becoming a circus clown.

In search of bents or in an honest effort to expose children to a variety of interests, we sometimes overprogram our children. In most communities, kids face a smorgasbord of extracurricular activities, such as Scouts, crafts, athletics, dancing, or computer camps. It's easy to overprogram and overwhelm children with too many activities. Then the disadvantage outweighs the advantage of helping them discover their bents.

At our house, we limit our children's activities, and with a little direction, they help weed out the choices. Sometimes midway through a session of lessons or a season of soccer, they know and we know this activity is not their bent. But we don't let them quit in the middle of a session. Because of their commitment they have to remain in the program for the duration of the session.

Some activities have nebulous durations. Take piano lessons for example. At age nine, our daughter begged to start piano lessons. We agreed. About a year later, she tired of the tedious practice time and wanted to quit and take flute in the school band.

We felt she should stick with the piano lessons long enough to get some lasting benefit from her investment of time and our investment of money. So we compromised. We didn't set a time frame, but we set a certain level of accomplishment as a goal. She had to reach the end of a certain book before she could quit. That gave her a goal and incentive. Music is not her bent, so we didn't continue to force her. But we tried to help her make the most of the experience.

SIBLINGS: SEPARATE AND DIFFERENT

Siblings are separate and uniquely different, and as parents we must be sensitive to these differences. Some parents claim they can feel the differences in their children even during pregnancies. One kicks; the other is quiet. One responds to movement and activity; another doesn't. One arrives on time; the other is two weeks late.

It didn't take us long to recognize the differences in our first two children. One had trouble falling asleep; the other slept easily and soundly. The same pattern is evident ten years later. One seems disorganized; the other has a penchant for organizing, getting up early, thinking things through, and making checklists of needs for the day's activities.

In part, some of these traits may be due to the way parents handle first and second children, but much, I am convinced, is due to their God-given bents. Traditionally, firstborn children who receive their parents' undivided attention are conservative and conforming. Because their parents have high expectations of them, they tend to be overachievers and perfectionists.

Second or middle children tend to be friendlier and less demanding. They are diplomatic and skilled at compromising. On the other hand, parents often are more reluctant to allow the baby or last child the freedom to grow up. Yet these children are usually charming, happy, and fun loving because they have been showered with affection.

We do our children no favors by comparing them with each other or expecting them to be just like a brother or sister. Black sheep in families may well be black sheep because they can't live up to the standards set by siblings. Because they come out of the same family mold, they feel they should keep up. Even worse, the parents feel they should.

Spacing of children in a family seems to affect the respect for separateness. "We had two children a year apart, and I found myself lumping the two of them together more than our other two who were born six years later and separated by four years," one mother said.

We must treat siblings differently out of respect for their uniqueness. When it comes to rules, this may be difficult because children have a keen memory. They remember exactly how old Tom was "when you let him go out on a date!" It's as if the pattern is cast in concrete with the first child. As parents we try to be fair with our children, but that doesn't mean we treat them exactly the same. Maybe the rules are the same, but we enforce them differently with each child.

Parents who bend over backward to treat each child fairly and equally often find their efforts backfire. I buy Lindsay a pair of shoes, so I feel I should buy Kendall a pair even though Kendall doesn't need shoes. Frantically, I try to keep track of Christmas presents to make sure we buy each child the same number. If they see me counting up this way, surely they will count too. Our efforts to be fair make them judge everything in terms of fairness. As discussed in the last chapter, life isn't fair.

Children of different ages may have different bedtimes. Children with different bents will bring home different grades on their report cards. My husband and I make an effort to read our children's report cards alone with each child instead of making the report card review a family affair.

We have to recognize that our children will not necessarily follow in our paths or each other's paths. They are not reflections of us or each other. They don't have to ditto our opinions, go to the same schools, or enter the same profession. Evelyn Bence, in her book *Leaving Home*, writes:

> *Many parents, blind to the separateness of their children, see that three must forever remain as one. Fathers are convinced that they are cutting a trail for their children to follow. Parents insist that children will finish all of college, whether they want to or not. Parents are deeply hurt when their children join a denomination different from theirs, molding the future into some shape other than what they had envisioned.*[3]

As parents, we prepare our children for independence and equip them to reach their maximum potential when we recognize and encourage their God-given gifts. We focus on their strengths not their weaknesses. We build their self-esteem as we help them grow up feeling good about the people they are becoming. We recognize that God is their creator, the architect, the potter, and the master planner.

We are the nurturers, temporarily entrusted with the responsibility of training them up and equipping them. Then because they are separate, because they are not possessions, we let them go.

CHAPTER 6

How to Let Go

"Blessed is the family where growing children are allowed to become what God would have them become as soon as possible, and blessed are the parents who encourage that to happen and as fast as they can, get out of the way."[1] That's a beatitude for parents from minister, author, and father, Charles Swindoll, who seems to understand how parents have trouble letting go and getting out of the way. Certain attitudes and habits trip us up and slow us down. Two of the common culprits are the way we worry and the way we assume our children's responsibilities.

Worry, I've decided, is an accepted part of a parent's job description. We worry about everything from their moral fiber to the amount of natural fiber in their diets. They say headache, we think CAT scan. They are fifteen minutes late, we think accident. They go off without a coat, we think pneumonia.

Worry is a major stumbling block to the smooth and simple release of our children. I hold on or protect because I don't want to worry. When I let go, I do so hesitantly, filled with the "what if" fears.

"O man of little faith," Jesus scolded Peter when he was afraid of the wind and the water, even in Jesus' presence. "Why did you doubt?" (Matt. 14:31 RSV). Our fears show a lack of faith. "To worry is a sin," I once heard. "It is taking on a responsibility that belongs to God."

One mother told me she could not truly let go of her children until she reached a maturity of faith that enabled her to claim the promise of Romans 8:28: "And we know that in all things God works for the good of those who love him, who have been called according to his purpose."

She finally translated that verse to mean that even if her son were struck by lightning on his way to school or even if her daughter had leukemia, she would be able to accept the irreversible situation, not happily but faithfully, knowing God would provide and bring good out of it. Romans 8:28 became the cornerstone of her faith, enabling her to let go.

One of the best ways to deal with fear is to look our worst fear right in the face. Probably my worst fear is the threat of losing one of my children. When I hesitate to let them do something, when I worry because they are late, when I say goodbye at the door, my worst fear is that they won't come back. What if something happened to one of them? How could I ever pick up the pieces and go on? Could I claim in faith Romans 8:28 ?

I've watched parents pick up the pieces. In fact, I've always been drawn to them in some magnetic way, knowing their experience could be my experience and searching for the assurance in their responses that I, too, could cope with what seems to be the worst possible disaster.

One good friend faced this situation just before Christmas last year, and her daily challenge now is to make sense out of life without her only son who was killed that clear, cold December afternoon. Just two hours earlier she had casually said goodbye to seventeen-year-old Kurt who went goose hunting with a friend. She reminded him to be home before dark. Since her husband was out of town and her daughter away at college, they were going to a favorite restaurant for dinner. Just the two of them. It would be a special treat.

The time passed quickly, but she remembers looking at the clock close to five and feeling that familiar twinge of fear she'd had since her children were toddlers. At dark she wants her family to gather into the safety of home from their various places.

A few minutes later the phone rang. It was the call she'd

dreaded all her life. "There has been an accident," the voice said. Her son . . . confusion of details. . . . Finally, the instructions, "Come to the hospital immediately."

By the time she got there, it was too late. Her son Kurt was dead, hit by a car as he crossed the road at dusk after hunting. At that moment, she began the nightmare of picking up the pieces. Along the way she often stopped to write down her feelings, memories, and prayers in the diary of her journey through despair, an open-hearted, broken-hearted conversation with a loving God. It's also the diary of a mother's reminiscences, a desperate grasping to pull together all the pieces because there will be no more memories. She wrote about the pain:

> *I feel I have a lifetime of love left for him and I don't know what to do with it. My heart is truly broken. Emotion that can't be controlled or conquered. I feel like I'm in a great ocean and You're holding my head above the water, and my friends have a hold of my hands, but I'm not able to come up because of the rock of sorrow that's tied to my ankles. The loss is so deep, there is no bottom.*

She wrote about her connected losses: Because Kurt, a junior in high school, was the only child at home, she suddenly lost her role as a mother.

> *You have to plan to separate from your children as they build their own lives and families, but the finality of death before you're ready is so hard to take.*
>
> *My whole life for the last 20 years has been at home, trying to teach my children right from wrong and what is pleasing in God's eyes and mine too. I feel a great need to focus my life in some new direction. My family really needs very little of me anymore.*

She wrote about her regrets that she worried too much and missed some of the joy of living with Kurt.

A mother's sense of responsibility is to guide, discipline, and shape, so she sometimes lacks the freedom to enjoy the child's exuberant gifts. Kurt's gifts were so apparent to others who approached him positively. Because of my anxiety, maybe I missed some of the joy of knowing him. I've always been an anxious mother, and it's a hard habit to break. Feelings can be so powerful. It was hard releasing him to grow up, to let God take some of the care.

She was surprised that she wasn't freed from that worry even after his death. Yet she sensed the Lord was leading her somewhere through the shadows of fear and doubt.

I don't know why. Nothing in this life can hurt him anymore. Help my heart to believe and know that he is okay, that he is resting in your love. I know you are teaching me to trust. I feel like I trusted you completely with my life, but now I know it wasn't an absolute trust. Help me to trust completely and learn your will for my life.

She began to realize she hadn't truly released Kurt to the Lord's loving protection even after death. One day a friend brought her a rose. It was a simple, thoughtful gesture, but she saw deeper significance in this rose.

Kurt had sometimes given her roses: one for her birthday and two last Valentine's Day. He'd surprised her sometimes, and she'd always been deeply touched. She felt the rose this day was sent by Kurt and God together for a purpose, and she decided to make her first trip back to the cemetery to put the rose on Kurt's grave. "It will symbolize God's great gift of you and my release of you into his care," she wrote before she went. "May my heart find the peace it so desperately needs. As the flower must not wither and die in my presence, so you left in the beauty and purity of youth."

It was New Year's Day. She drove to the cemetery and sat alone on the fresh grave. She thought, prayed, and finally wrote:

Our children never really belong to us. They are God's from the beginning and only loaned to us for whatever length of time and whatever eternal purpose God has in mind. And yet, they are truly a part of our very life and being. Losing one is worse than losing an arm or leg. Only trusting that God is their true source and true ending can bring any peace of mind. Trust and faith are tested to the utmost. May my faith and trust be strengthened.

I return what was never really mine, but still a part of me—a very part of my body after conception. After birth all we ever really have are images and memories from moment to moment when loved ones are out of sight. It's funny that the moment and memories never seem so important until you know the time to build any more has passed. Let me see the importance of each moment, cherish each special time.

I miss him terribly and know there will always be a part of me missing, but I know you have something more planned for my life. I thank you for using Kurt's life and death for good. Please use mine to your glory; let me serve you in whatever way, grand or small.

That day she released her son to the Lord. She still has a broken heart. She still knows she will never be the same person. But in her journey through despair, she is seeing old Scripture in a new light. "In all things, God works for good. . . ." Maybe the good won't be tomorrow or even next year. Maybe the good will be in eternity, she thinks.

"Weeping may tarry for the night, but joy comes with the morning" (Ps. 30:5 RSV). Maybe the joy won't be the kind she's known before. Maybe it will be a different joy. In her diary, she concludes:

Love costs, but it's worth the price. Having Kurt in my life for seventeen years is worth every minute of the pain I feel now. His life was a precious gift; his presence an irreplaceable treasure. He is safely home, and God will help me complete my journey here. There are worse things than death.

Job looked his worst fears in the face. He lost the things he cherished the most: his children, his wealth, and his health. His friends condemned him. But Job came through his incredible suffering, rejoicing in the Lord.

The first night our son Derek was in the hospital with diabetes, a Christian friend called, "I know this may sound funny," she said, "but I almost envy you the journey you're about to embark upon with the Lord." I thought it sounded absurd at the moment but now I know what she meant. We are most dependent on the Lord during times of crises. Even a journey through despair becomes a meaningful experience when we walk with the Lord. He turns our challenges into opportunities: our suffering brings growth.

I am not thankful our son has diabetes. I'm sure the Lord didn't will it for him. But I'm thankful the Lord has given him the courage to accept it, the strength to deal with the daily injections, and the maturing faith not to fear the future.

When we face a loss, these are the questions we ask: Is God sufficient? Can we let go of a spouse, a child, or perfect health? Can we be stripped of all these securities and know that God is enough?

Job did. Kurt's mother is on that journey of growth. Others have reached that understanding and inspire us to stop our worrying to give our children the freedom to go and grow with confidence, to make choices, and even to fail at times.

LET OUR CHILDREN GO AND GROW WITH CONFIDENCE

As parents, we all struggle with the nagging daily decisions of whether we should allow our children to take the bus to town, to see a movie with friends, or to go skiing with the neighbors. We're anxious as we watch them jump off the high diving board, drive off in the family car, or go rafting in whitewater. All of these activities carry with them an element of risk, and we find ourselves faced again with fears. These fears tempt us to try to control their environment. Then we limit their experiences and their growth.

"Every time I send my daughter out the door for the ski team racing practice, my heart is in my throat," a friend told me. "But I just have to remember: There is something I can do. I can always pray."

I know another mother who sends her children off to school or any other outing daily after mentally dressing them in the whole armor of God as vividly described in Ephesians 6:10–20. She claims the promise of protection by giving each child the belt of truth, the breastplate of righteousness, shoes of readiness, the shield of faith, the helmet of salvation, and the sword of the Spirit.

Still another mother prays for angels to surround her children. We equip our children to handle challenges and then we send them out the door with confidence and a prayer.

"From the moment we awake until we fall asleep, we must commend our loved ones wholly and unreservedly to God and leave them in his hands, transforming our anxiety then into prayers on their behalf," writes Dietrich Bonhoeffer in *Letters and Papers From Prison*.[2]

Parenting carries with it an element of risk. We have to accept the results of the decisions we make or actions we take with our children. For weeks, Kurt's mother agonized over her decision to let him go hunting that afternoon. What if she had said no? What if she had told him to be home earlier? Yet she began to see the futility of reliving the event and she knew she hadn't caused the accident to happen. Prayerfully, she had to let go of that attitude.

I think of the risks Moses' mother Jochebed faced as she put three-month-old baby Moses in the basket of bulrushes and floated him down the river. Yet she had to take a risk to save him from certain death at the hands of Pharaoh, who had commanded that all sons born to Hebrews should be killed. What courage it took to let baby Moses float away to an unknown destiny in the river. What rewards she received because she had the faith to take the risk. Moses was discovered by Pharaoh's daughter, who took pity on him and even hired Moses' own mother to take care of him until he grew old enough to live with Pharaoh's daughter (Exod. 2:1–10).

We encourage our children's independence as we encourage them to be curious and enthusiastic about life's opportunities and activities. We discourage that independence if we communicate our fears to them.

WE MUST GIVE OUR CHILDREN THE FREEDOM TO MAKE CHOICES AND ACCEPT THE CONSEQUENCES OF THEIR DECISIONS

So much of life is based on choices: What shall I wear? Which cereal shall I have for breakfast? Which chore shall I tackle first? In an effort to build confidence in their ability to make choices, we begin allowing children to make simple choices with minimal consequences when they are young. As they grow, our role becomes advisory. We help them look at their options and consider the pros and cons of each. Our goal is to teach them how to think not what to think. And the more we allow them to think for themselves, the more they care about what we think. They learn we won't force them to think what we think. We listen to their opinions and ideas and let them make choices for themselves.

Sometimes even hearing our opinions may be difficult. "Please don't tell me what you think, Mom," a fourteen-year-old boy pleaded with his mother. "I have a hard time separating it from what I think."

A college freshman who had gained confidence in his own decisions called home one day for some advice. "I'd like your opinion," he told his parents, "but I want you to know that in the end, I'm going to make up my own mind, and you may not agree with my decision." By the time our children leave home, our role is to offer opinions as asked and to accept their decisions.

WE MUST GIVE OUR CHILDREN THE FREEDOM TO FAIL

Tempting as it is, we should not protect our children from failure. Their lives, like ours, are shaped more by failure than by success, more by pain than by joy. "Consider it pure joy, my brothers, whenever you face trials of many kinds, because you know that the testing of your faith develops perseverance" (James 1:2–3). Trials and suffering strengthen the soul. If we stand by our children with love and support, they will learn from their failures, even as the Prodigal Son did. The boy took his inheritance and left home. His father knew he couldn't cope with that much money and that much freedom. Sure enough, the boy squandered his money in loose living and soon was penniless and hungry. How much his father must have wanted to help his son out. But he didn't. As a result, the son learned from his experience and returned home to ask his father's forgiveness.

"Please give me the freedom to make decisions concerning myself. Permit me to fail, so that I can learn from my mistakes. Then someday I'll be prepared to make the kind of decisions life requires of me," writes Dr. Kevin Leman in his "Child's Ten Commandments to Parents" from his book *Parenthood Without Hassles—Well Almost.*[3]

WE MUST LET GO OF ASSUMING THEIR RESPONSIBILITIES

Because we love our children, we too often assume responsibilities that are rightfully theirs. Take this typical example. It is the early morning rush hour at our house. The digital clock on the stove reads out the seconds and minutes until 8:06, "blast-off time," when the school bus arrives. The kids are wolfing down their cereal; the dog is barking to be fed; lunch boxes are clanging open and closed; and there is the frenzied, last-minute search for books, homework papers, jump ropes, gloves, and the polished rock for Show and Tell. Suddenly, it's time, and with one final flurry, the kids are out the door. A few minutes later, as I sweep up the crumbs, I discover one child has left the homework paper she worked so hard to do the night before.

Summed up in the presence of that piece of paper on the counter is a major challenge of letting go. What do I do about it? Ideally, the answer is . . . nothing.

And nothing is the hardest thing to do. My maternal heart hurts to think of the disappointment she'll feel when she realizes she has forgotten it and the embarrassment she'll suffer when she tells the teacher. After all, I do have time to brush my hair, get my shoes, jump in the car, and deliver the paper to school before class starts.

Why do I do nothing? Simply because I should not assume responsibility for the mistake and therefore change the consequences. I must let go of my instinct to take the paper to school so she will learn to assume responsibility for her papers in the future. It's a crucial step in the cognitive learning process.

Also, if I allow her to experience the consequences of this action, it frees me from the responsibility of nagging her or reminding her of the mistake. I don't need to say "I told you so!", which is always tempting. I don't need to nag, "Now I told you to put your homework paper in your school bag as soon as you finished it. If you has done what I told you, you would not have forgotten it!" Kids don't need to hear that. They know it, especially if we don't chase after them with their papers but allow them to suffer the consequences of going to class without their homework.

There is an exception to this rule that a young Christian mother shared with me. "Sometimes I take the forgotten lunch box, book, or paper to school for them," she said, "and I use it as a chance to explain the meaning of grace. They know they forgot it and didn't deserve to have it delivered to them. Similarly God showers us with His grace, His loving kindness, and compassion freely and consistently even though we don't deserve it. Grace is unreserved love that is given with no thought of reward."

In her book *Traits of a Healthy Family,* author Delores Curran encourages parents to allow their children to assume responsibilities because irresponsible children grow into irresponsible adults. Healthy families "tend to insist that members take full responsibility for their actions and doing that means living with the consequences of irresponsibility," she writes. "Our real responsibility as parents is to offer them the opportunity to grow in responsibility, not assume their responsibilities because they are our children."[4]

At our house we try to determine who owns the problem or who is responsible for it. Let's take as an example looking for a lost shoe. "Where is my shoe?" a child demands, close to blast-off time in the morning.

"I don't know," I answer, opening the closet door to search for the shoe. With the act of looking in the closet, I begin to own the problem and I assume the responsibility for it. Since the child is no dummy, he sits down and lets me look for the shoe. Obviously, something is wrong here. The lost shoe is not my problem. It is his problem, but if I claim ownership or assume responsibility, he can quit looking.

Our twelve-year-old son wears a retainer. The orthodontist tells him to wear it at all times except when eating or exercising. During his monthly visits, the doctor can tell how much progress he's making and consequently how much he's been wearing it. I used to attend these sessions with him, and the doctor's scolding made me uncomfortable. So I constantly nagged and reminded Derek to wear the retainer.

I suddenly realized this wasn't my problem. It was Derek's. He is old enough to shoulder the responsibility himself. I surprised him when I told him I would no longer nag him, but I also would no longer accept the consequences. He would have to go to the appointments alone. I had been the insulating buffer between Derek and the doctor. I had intercepted the doctor's response. When I no longer accompanied him, he owned the problem and began wearing the retainer more often.

Ownership of some problems is fuzzier. One Halloween, I spent a lot of time getting together a great Orphan Annie costume for our kindergartner: the red and white dress, long white socks, the black patent leather shoes, and even a perfect, curly iridescent red wig. Just before the all-school parade, however, Kendall had a change of heart. She didn't want to be Annie. She said the wig was "dumb" and she refused to participate. She cried; I was angry. Then the words echoed in my mind. "Is it her problem or your problem?" She had no problem. She was content to sit this one out. Her refusal became my problem because I wanted to see her in the parade.

In determining ownership of a problem, Barbara Coloroso, a nationally known expert on the subject of discipline, tells parents to ask two questions: Is it life-threatening or morally-threatening? If the answer is yes, parents should intervene. If not, the problem belongs to the child.

Apply this principle to the problem of cleanliness in a child's room. I have a natural sense of orderliness that our son did not inherit. Our ideas of clean differ considerably. He is perfectly happy to live knee-deep in clutter that offends me; but I don't have to live in it. By closing the door, I don't even have to look at it. It isn't life-threatening or morally-threatening to his future. Nobody dies from a dirty room, so it is his problem. I did keep one part that becomes my problem since I still do his laundry. So if his clothes get dirty on the floor, I have to assume the consequences, and doing laundry is one of my least favorite household duties. Therefore, the natural solution is to put a hamper in his room, and let him start doing his own laundry. Then he will totally own the problem.

If we let go of assuming their responsibilities, we must also let go of our rigid, uncompromising standards. If we give them responsibilities such as keeping their rooms clean, we must allow the outcomes: We let them make their beds in spite of the lumps; We let them do the dishes even though we could do it faster and better. The results will be less than perfect, but we need to compromise our standards and expectations.

Our goal is to teach them to assume responsibilities as they grow up because the fruits of irresponsibility can render a child incapable of coping with homework, demands of a job, or even commitment to marriage. All of which may be goals we have for them as as we let go.

CHAPTER 7

Building a Firm Foundation

When I was learning to play competitive tennis several years ago, my patient but sometimes exasperated coach would stop me midstroke and sternly tell me to go back to basics. It made me mad, but she was always right. If I was getting sloppy or not executing the strokes correctly, it was merely a matter of forgetting the fundamentals. Her philosophy was simple: If I wanted to be a good tennis player, I needed to build my competence upon a firm foundation of basic skills.

Raising and releasing children operates much the same way. If we want our children to become strong, we must build strength into them by giving them a firm foundation of values early in life. This foundation becomes the footing upon which all future knowledge is built in the cognitive learning process. This foundation roots them and guides them through the temptations, assaults, and challenges of life.

Jesus told the multitudes about the wise man who built his house on rock, "The rain came down, the streams rose, and the winds blew and beat against that house; yet it did not fall, because it had its foundation on the rock" (Matt. 7:25). Not so for the foolish man who built his house on sand; the same ravages assaulted his less secure house, and "it fell with a great crash" (Matt. 7:27).

I once heard this firm foundation described as the "core

theory." According to this theory, kids come in two categories: apples and onions. An apple has a core: the tough, fibrous, seedy center that remains even if the outside skin or flesh is bruised or chipped away. An onion, on the other hand, has no core. When an onion is peeled away, nothing remains.

Continuing with this analogy, kids with cores may be bruised or torn by life's experiences, but no matter how many mistakes they make they will always get back on track because their value system remains intact. A counselor friend summed it up a different way: If our kids are basically good up through sixth grade, no matter how rebellious or difficult they become in adolescence, eventually they will emerge again as good kids. Their cores will carry them through.

I'm sure God wants us to raise kids with cores. He wants us to plant the seeds of Christian values deep within their tender souls when they are young and pliable. As they grow, these values give them structure and strength to withstand the ravages of their environment.

The ingredients of a firm foundation are the values that shape their attitudes about God, self, and others. God is their spiritual foundation; self is the strength and confidence that grows out of the recognition and acceptance of God's love; and a sense of others is the way they treat the people around them. It is the manifestation of their understanding of grace, compassion, loyalty, and commitment that grows primarily out of their family relationships. As parents, we use a combination of tools to mold and shape these attitudes in our children. We transmit values mainly through our loving them, teaching them, disciplining them, and modeling for them.

GOD

God is ever present, always the same yesterday, today, and tomorrow, and utterly predictable. When I was growing up and facing constant changes in my body and my life, God became my security in my moody, confusing world. From the singsong routine of childlike prayers and faith, I felt a growing sense of the Lord within the core of my being.

According to a recent poll, the greatest threat to American family life is the absence of a "religious and spiritual foundation." One of the 200,000 respondents said, "If God were put first, fewer problems would be encountered in our lives. A strong belief in God and the unity that exists when worshipping Him together helps give meaning and direction to family life!"[1]

SELF

A sense of self is the child's realization first that he or she is an individual who is separate and different from a parent and then, that he or she is an individual loved by God. "Jesus Loves Me . . . " sings the child, and on the basis of this knowledge, he or she begins to build the fragile, crucial sense of self-worth. Feeling good about oneself is self-esteem, a quality most experts agree is necessary for a child's development. Healthy self-esteem gives a strong sense of security to a child. Learning to love oneself precedes learning to love others.

This concept applies to adults as well as children. In everyday situations, I am not free to love others when I don't feel good about myself. I can't concentrate on someone else's needs when I am feeling self-conscious and worried about myself. If my jeans feel too tight, my fingernails too short, and my hair disheveled, I don't reach out with much warmth to the new neighbor I see in the grocery store. I'm in bondage to my unlovable sense of self at that moment.

OTHERS

How a child treats others directly reflects of how he or she is treated, and this behavior usually serves as a true barometer of the personality under construction. "You can tell a lot about a guy from the way he treats his dog and his sister," my husband keeps telling our children. They have heard that proverb so many times that I'm sure the impact is diluted, but the truth is still there. We reflect our values and attitudes by the way we live and treat others.

Thank heavens God gave us families that serve as microcosms of the real world, yet they give us more love, support, and security than the real world. Families provide the ideal niches for laboratory experiments in the lessons of life, especially in relationships with others. Every emotion imaginable is felt and magnified within the family unit: love, anger, greed, impatience, pride, and jealousy. Yet the family structure teaches loyalty, forgiveness, compassion, and commitment: all cornerstones of a firm foundation in learning to get along with others.

A sense of family is vitally important to a growing child. To prepare our children for release, we must first establish this important sense of family, the secure homebase from which they are launched. A sense of family is the nebulous but strong glue that welds people together in a single unit.

From this sense of family comes shared pride through knowing the traditions, patterns of speech, and systems of operations that make the unit function. For example: At our house we always say grace before we eat; At our house we get five dollars allowance, but we buy our own school lunches; At our house we always have doughnuts on Saturday mornings; and At our house we celebrate family birthdays with balloons and presents at breakfast.

Each family has a junk drawer in a different place, a different system for disposing of old newspapers and aluminum cans, and different rules about the television, the telephone, and even the toothpaste. These may be insignificant rules or systems within themselves, but it is the knowledge of them that causes the feeling of belonging in a family and establishes a bonding loyalty between members.

LOVE

We build foundations with love. We transmit attitudes about God, self, and others by the way we love our children. From the day they come into our lives, our children sense our communication of love. In their first conscious moments they absorb emotions. No wonder increasing numbers of families are demanding more intimate birthing experiences where bonding is natural and uninhibited. According to studies, a child's sense of security and trust is established within the first few months of life. As important as nutrition is the nurturing sense of love.

Our relationship with our children models the relationship we have with our heavenly Father. Our love should be like His love: unconditional, consistent, and full of grace. Our children need to understand that they don't earn our love, just as we don't earn our salvation. Our love is not based on their performance, which is a relief, because children are known to perform badly. At least ours do. Already in their young lives, they have spilled hundreds of glasses of milk, shared family secrets with strangers, and broken a few family heirlooms. They fight with each other while an acquaintance is complimenting me on an article I wrote about the joys of family life. They make messes, embarrass me, and disappoint me. Still, I love them and I take it for granted that they know that.

Yet I'm surprised to see how relieved and comforted they are to hear these words: "There is nothing you can say or do that will ever change my love for you. I may be disappointed, angry, or hurt, but I will never, never love you less." It's a message they begin to believe because it is repeated in actions and words, and it brings them a lot closer to understanding God's grace and forgiving love.

Our love is manifested in many ways. It is both tough and tender. Sometimes it means hugs and kisses. Other times it means some form of discipline; but usually it is the sensitive combination of both.

Tough love, a popular term, means giving up a short-term benefit in hopes of reaching a long-term goal. It means teaching children to be accountable and accept the consequences of their actions. We sacrifice the comfort of pleasing our children at the moment in an effort to teach them an important lesson in life. We do what's good for them in the long run.

We say no to the three-year-old who whines for cookies before dinner. Even though cookies would make him happy, saying no is better for him. We demand that our children finish out the season on the swim team, even though quitting would please them. Although the practices are tougher than they anticipated, not quitting teaches them something about commitments.

When our son was diagnosed diabetic, his doctor encouraged us to send him away to a weeklong camp for diabetics where he would meet other children who shared his problem, learn more about diabetes control, and gain confidence in his ability to take care of himself. At age nine he did not want to go. But we gently and firmly insisted because we believed the camp experience would be an important step toward independence.

The night before he was to leave, we were stuffing clothes into his duffle bag. His voice began to quiver, "I know you can't change it now, but why are you making me go?" he asked with tears in his eyes.

We'd been through the reasons a hundred times, and my heart was breaking for him as he anticipated the homesickness. It would have been so easy to call the whole thing off at that moment; it would be so difficult to drive him to camp in the morning.

"When you walk away," he stammered, trying to control himself, "I will feel terrible." I prayed that night and the next day for angels to surround him and for the strength to walk away.

The sun was bright that June morning, and we left the suddenly small, brave figure on the steps of a rickety camp cabin. With a quick hug, I turned and took a long walk away. I endured a week that was almost as hard on me as it was on him. That was tough love.

We look back now and know the camp experience was good for our son. In fact, I believe camp experiences beginning in late elementary school are good for all children because they learn to cope away from home. Children should not face the challenge of college as their first venture away from home.

Love also allows for individuality. We don't love each of our children in the same way at the same time. They are uniquely different, and we deal positively with their differences to build their self-esteem and confidence. Kids continually ask themselves, "Am I okay?" We need to affirm them because what they think of themselves is based on how they think others see them. When they are young, we are the mirrors that reflect their sense of self. We reinforce their positive images of themselves. They become what we encourage them to become.

In an article entitled "What Your Kids Really Want," writer Phyllis Theroux writes, "Admittedly you can't give children everything they want, but when I reflect upon what they want the most, I think it is to feel that they are good—deep down, where maybe no one else, including themselves, can see it."[2] That is not only what they want most; it is what they need most.

TEACH

We give our children a firm foundation in relating to God, to themselves, and to others by teaching them properly. As parents, we are their first and most important teachers. We tell them stories, read to them, use examples, and give instruction, which we reinforce through discipline and modeling. Our children are like sponges, absorbing what they see and hear, especially when they are little. That's why our influence upon them is so critically important when their foundations are under construction and their minds are so able to absorb what we teach them.

We teach by talking to them. We tell them, for instance, that God made families because he believes families are important. He put the first four people into a family: Adam and Eve, and their sons Cain and Abel. Because God knew this family would face struggles, as would all families throughout time, He gave them rules to live by that He also wants us to live by today. He tells parents to love their children and to teach them to obey; he tells children to obey their parents.

We tell them our family rules and teach them to remember those rules. Since our children were babies, my husband Lynn has told them we have three rules in our house that are variations of Scripture, communicated in our own lingo. The Number One Rule is "Never tell a lie." It comes, he explains to me, from "to thine own self be true" and includes being honest to God, self, and others. The Number Two Rule is "Think of others." This comes from "love thy neighbor." The Number Three Rule is "Don't forget where you came from." This is the family loyalty oath that means our children might fight behind closed doors, but once out in the world whether on the school bus, playground, or ski slope, they stick together and help one another.

Lynn can stop our children midsentence or midaction and ask, "What is the Number One Rule in this house?" Immediately they recognize the infraction and repeat the rule.

Children have an incredible capacity for memorization that is a potential we don't maximize. Our children sing countless popular tunes or repeat television commercials verbatim. Repetition enables them to memorize, and memorization is a powerful tool.

Bob Biehl, president of Masterplanning Associates and nationally known for his creative techniques in transmitting values, has come up with a unique system to help children learn family values. He suggests that using language appropriate for the age of the children, parents draw up a list of values considered most critical. Making the list presents a challenge, but the benefit comes in having children memorize the concepts in sets of five and in rewarding them for their success. The list may have up to fifty values, including simple Scriptures or familiar sayings. The possibilities are endless. So is the potential of the system.[3]

We equip our children to meet challenges by helping them memorize Scripture, especially short, meaningful verses. "I can do all things through Christ who strengthens me," one youngster kept telling himself as his knees knocked together while standing on the starting block in the first swim meet. "The Lord is my strength and my shield; in him my heart trusts," a child repeated to herself as she walked home alone at dusk.

Author Elisabeth Elliot claims, "I was raised on Scripture the way some kids are raised on vitamins." Children memorize verses not only because they repeat them, but also because they see them in writing. I keep a supply of 3 x 5 cards handy on which to jot appropriate Scripture or inspirational sayings that I post on any visible spot such as the refrigerator or window sill. Some families use a similar card system to memorize a Scripture a week, repeating it and talking about it at breakfast or dinner. Christian book stores sell simple card systems that promote memorization of Scripture.

The spiritual foundation we give our children early in life will become the cornerstone of their own personal faith. "Lead your children to Christ," Jill Briscoe told mothers at a women's conference. "Don't let someone else do it for you and rob you of the pleasure of being there when they accept the Lord Jesus."

We lead our children to Christ by teaching them the Word and making Jesus real in their lives.

> *And these words which I command you this day shall be upon your heart; and you shall teach them diligently to your children, and shall talk of them when you sit in your house, and when you walk by the way, and when you lie down, and when you rise (Deut. 6:6–7 RSV).*

I used to have a problem with this Scripture. I felt I had to dance around every sunbeam in the living room, inanely blessing every object because God made it, and spouting Scripture at every turn. If I did that, I'd soon lose my credibility with our children. Obviously that's an exaggerated translation of the Scripture, and it misses the meaning. Larry Christenson in *The Christian Family* translates this Scripture to mean "a quiet threading of God's Word through the warp and woof of family life."[4] I like that interpretation because it tells us to be *real* and relevant when telling our children about God.

We try to make the Lord real in our children's lives by talking with Him through prayer, sharing with them how He works in our lives, and seizing upon the potential of a moment to translate Scripture into action or to recognize the power of the Lord. I remember one particularly vivid instance when Lindsay knew that God had heard our prayer.

She was eight years old and just learning to ski. At the end of her first day of lessons, she was anxious to show me what she'd learned, so I took her up the chair lift for the last run of the day. We headed for a beginners' slope, plainly marked by large, green signs, but somehow I took the wrong cutoff and we found ourselves hopelessly in the middle of an expert slope with nowhere to go but down.

We teetered on the brink of what looked like a cliff, carved by treacherously deep moguls. Only a mother and novice skier like me would understand the sheer terror I felt at that moment.

"I can't do this, Mom," Lindsay stated in a quiet voice. That was an understatement. I knew she couldn't do it and I seriously doubted that I could do it.

The slope was deserted. I wasn't surprised. *Who would take a slope like this on purpose?* I wondered. "Let's pray, Lindsay," I said automatically because I was totally helpless.

Pray we did, and within seconds two ski patrolmen schussed into sight above us. They could read the panic in my body language. "Need any help?" one asked.

Our problem was no problem to them. One took Lindsay's poles; the other simply put her small form between his legs, held on to her, and expertly threaded his way down through the valley of moguls to the bottom of the hill. The grace of God got me down behind them, and the experience gave me a chance to tell Lindsay that I don't believe in coincidences or good luck and that God sent those ski patrolmen to us in answer to prayer. Three years later, we still talk about the day God sent us two angels in ski patrolmen outfits. It was a day the living God was real in our lives.

DISCIPLINE

The word "discipline" has such negative connotations. When it is surrounded by such verbs as "love," "teach," and "model," it stands out as the bad guy, harsh and unpleasant. Yet the Bible is filled with verses about the rewards of discipline and the parent's responsibility of disciplining a child. Even as an adult, I know that a life without discipline is not a happy one.

"No discipline seems pleasant at the time, but painful.

Later on, however, it produces a harvest of righteousness and peace for those who have been trained by it" (Heb. 12:11). The goal of discipline is to teach obedience and self-control. If we teach our children to be obedient to us when they are young, they will learn to be obedient to God as they mature. In learning to submit to parents, children actually learn to submit to a will higher than their own.

Samuel's quick obedience to Eli was the fruit of his mother's early training. The little boy obeyed and assisted Eli and quickly responded in the middle of the night when he thought Eli was calling him. "A child's relationship to Jesus thrives in direct relation to the obedience which he gives to his parents," writes Larry Christenson in *The Christian Family.* "Jesus lives and works in the life of an obedient child."[5]

Consistent discipline gives children a sense of security because it sets limits and creates a basically predictable environment. In a predictable environment children can meet new challenges confidently. Proper discipline rewards and reinforces good behavior and discourages bad behavior. It develops the sense of conscience from within that teaches children to respond to right and wrong independently.

Our heavenly Father wants us to discipline our children as he lovingly disciplines us: firmly, fairly, and consistently. If we don't discipline our children, we suffer the unpleasant consequences with them. The Bible is filled with stories of real people who illustrate this point. King David, himself a sinner with Bathsheba, grew sloppy in administering discipline to his sons Ammon and Absalom. He failed to discipline them. Subsequently, Absalom put Ammon to death and then later turned on his father David.

Discipline should be firm. We say what we mean and we mean what we say. Often in a fit of anger or impatience, I threaten a child with consequences I know I can't or won't carry out. Before a family outing, one child keeps teasing another child. "Stop bugging your sister, or you won't go with us" I tell him. I don't mean that. He has to go with us. I don't have a baby-sitter and I'm not willing to stay home with the child. I lose my effectiveness if I say what I don't mean.

Discipline should be fair. The apostle Paul defines the parents' responsibilities in disciplining their children: "Fathers, do not provoke your children to anger, but bring them up in the discipline and instruction of the Lord" (Eph. 6:4 RSV). The punishment has to fit the crime. A child should not be spanked for an honest mistake nor should he be abused through discipline. "Fathers, do not embitter your children, or they will become discouraged" (Col. 3:21). If discipline is excessive and unfair, a child will grow up lacking self-confidence.

Discipline should be consistent. We have a responsibility to run our house as much like the real world as possible to prepare our children to live in the world. Parents should agree on the rules and enforce them together. Consistently we teach our children there are logical, predictable consequences for their actions. At age three if they deliberately disobey, the consequences may be a spanking. At age six if they do not make their beds, they may not be allowed to play.

Their actions and our actions bring about consequences in the real world. If dad gets caught driving 50 miles per hour in a 30-mile-per-hour zone, he gets a ticket. If Mom is on a diet but nibbles cookies all day long, she will gain instead of lose weight. The other day, I heard about a woman in our neighborhood who got involved in a love affair. She watched her marriage dissolve and her children suffer physically and emotionally. These were the consequences of her actions.

MODELING

We transmit values to our children most effectively by the way we live our lives. What we do speaks louder than what we say, and our children do as they see done. Observe how they mimic us: the way the hands go on the hips; the tone of voice in disciplining dolls. Even their bad habits are usually our bad habits. Our son is a master at procrastination. And why not? He lives with two great teachers, his mom and dad.

We have great power over and impact upon our children by our actions. One of the most memorable television commercials I've ever seen uses that premise. It is a thirty-second, anti-smoking spot sponsored by the American Heart Association—a commercial with few words, but a powerful message. It opens with a little boy and his daddy walking through the woods together on a bright, sunny day. As they walk, the boy keeps looking up at his father adoringly, trying to imitate his every move.

First the little guy adjusts his identical hat to the same cockeyed angle, stuffs his fists in his pockets, and throws stones into a pond, just like Daddy. Finally the two sit down together under a shady tree, the little boy still watching his father intently. Just then Dad pulls out a pack of cigarettes, lights one up, leans back, and tosses the pack down in the grass beside his son. The little boy looks down at the cigarettes, then looks back up at his daddy with a smile, the same hero worship still in his eyes.

"A Child Learns What He Lives" is the familiar inspirational piece often seen on wall hangings in pediatrician's offices or children's rooms. It begins "If a child lives with criticism, he learns to condemn; If a child lives with hostility, he learns to fight . . ." and ends with "If a child lives with security, he learns to have faith; If a child lives with approval, he learns to like himself; If a child lives with acceptance and friendship, he learns to find love in the world."

I'm not a perfect parent. I don't always model godly responses. I often perform badly. I get angry; I make mistakes; I lose my patience; and I act selfishly. As our children grow up, they are more keenly aware of these faults and hold me more accountable for "walking my talk." That's why I see modeling as a continual challenge for parents. But modeling is also a powerful tool. While living with us, our children learn that God loves and works through less-than-perfect people.

CHAPTER 8

Early Training Rules

Before our first child was born, Lynn and I promised each other that a new baby would not change our lives. We would not under any circumstances become like the boring and overzealous parents we knew who talked of nothing else but babies. In public we would not act like our baby was the best baby in the whole world. And finally we would not give up evenings out together, move all our knickknacks out of reach, or in any other way let this baby totally rule our lives.

That was before we had our baby.

It didn't take long before our baby proved how naïve we were. His first night home from the hospital, he skillfully took control and began to rule our lives. For the first few hours home, he slept peacefully and I was just beginning to feel like Cinderella, playing house with our new little family when our cherub woke up and shattered my fairy tale. He started screaming as if something were life-threatening, and we thought surely he was trying to tell us something. We knew nothing. In our prenatal classes, we learned everything about labor and delivery, but we forgot to learn anything about taking care of a newborn.

So between the hours of 10 P.M. and 5 A.M., Lynn and I took an on-the-job crash course in parenting. We read all our books. Unable to understand why he was crying when obviously we were meeting all his needs, we alternately rocked, changed, fed, burped, and again changed this helpless infant. The more we passed him back and forth, the more he cried; he was the guinea pig of our inexperience and he let us know he was not pleased.

We emerged from that night bleary-eyed but baptized by fire into the world of parenting. Only time and experience finally taught us this fragile infant wouldn't break; he could finish a nap with wet diapers; and best of all, he could cry himself to sleep without any permanent emotional damage. For the first few weeks, however, we were engaged in a major control battle aimed at teaching him that for everything there is a time: a time to wake up, a time to sleep, a time to eat, and a time to be quietly contented. He didn't give in easily.

During our adjustment to parenthood, we immersed ourselves in child-rearing information. We talked to friends, attended seminars, read how-to books, and listened to TV talk shows. We overdosed on the subject, and I was left with two lasting dislikes.

My first dislike is the familiar compare-the-baby conversations that are variations of the "best baby in the world" attitude. In spite of our pre-baby vows, we were drawn into these conversations that seemed to occur whenever two or more parents gathered together. Inevitably the talk turned to whose baby slept through the night first, got the first tooth, or said the first "Dada." Somehow these accomplishments seemed more appropriate for the sheets of the "Baby Book of Milestones" than for discussion topics over coffee; yet, these conversations have followed us all the way through grade school. Only the feats change with who started reading first, who learned to swim first, or who accepted the responsibility of a newspaper route first.

These conversations gave me the first taste of what it felt like to wrap my ego around my child's accomplishments, even though I had nothing to do with the appearance of the first tooth. Compare-the-baby conversations made me uncomfortable because they implied these milestones were directly related to superior brain power, realized or potential. But I knew better: The truth is all children are unique and develop at different rates.

My other dislike is the hopeless, helpless feeling that no matter where I stand in the timetable of my children's lives, it's too late to change the lasting impact of past mistakes. Some things in life will never be theirs because I did not eat enough wheat germ when I was pregnant, did not read enough to them when they were toddlers, or model enough patience when they were preschoolers. But now it's too late.

Finally though, I've come to the peaceful conclusion that it's never too late to have an impact on our children's lives. As long as the Lord gives us one more conversation, one more moment together, or for parents of children who have grown and left home, even one more letter, phone conversation or prayer, it's never too late to make a difference in the lives of our children. In that spirit, we will explore some ideas about the independence and letting go of our children at different age levels.

ZERO TO TWO YEARS OLD

Major changes have taken place in the preparation for birth and the birth experience over the last several years that definitely affect the attachment between parent and child. The most important changes are natural childbirth, the father's participation in the childbirth experience, and the surging interest in the bonding process between parents and child after the birth.

When I was born, neither of my parents was immediately aware of my arrival. My father was down the hall asleep in a waiting room, and my mother was under anesthesia. I don't think it has had any lifelong effects on my emotional well-being, but it probably slowed down their bonding to me, especially my father's since he always thought that taking care of babies was women's work.

I know from my own experience that bonding takes place when mother, father, and child are together immediately after birth especially if they have the freedom to caress or nurse the newborn. When Derek was born twelve years ago, I had to talk the doctor into allowing Lynn into the delivery room at the last minute, and I think he consented only because he feared I would get hysterical if he refused. It was a new idea at that hospital.

We both watched the incredible miracle of the birth. After Derek was born at nearly 10:00 P.M., we only got one good look at him before he was whisked away to the nursery. Lynn was shooed out of the room shortly after that, and I was left alone, exhausted but wide awake, to sort out my thoughts and wonder about that stranger in the nursery down the hall who would forever be part of our lives. The umbilical cord had been cut. Suddenly, after being intricately bound together for nine months, we were separate and alone, and I felt confused and ambivalent about our new relationship.

I didn't hold Derek until the next morning, and for three days he was brought to me only for short periods to nurse. By the time we got home, I didn't feel very confident or comfortable with him. Our next two babies slept in bassinets next to my bed in the hospital, and I could cuddle or feed them whenever I wanted. I felt I knew them when we carried them home.

Fathers play a major supportive role in helping during labor and delivery these days. I've even heard couples announce: "We are pregnant." Together they endure the nine months, God's perfect amount of time to prepare both babies and parents for the arrival. Couples take childbirth classes together where dad learns to act as the coach, who does a whole lot more than boil water and tear sheets during labor and delivery. He participates from start to finish in this intensely intimate experience that not only bonds father to child but husband to wife as he understands and appreciates the woman's role in this miracle. The father who watches the birth of his son or daughter reports that he immediately feels tied to his baby. Bonding is important.

For the first several months, the baby is totally dependent upon the parents for everything. This is the 100 percent part of the scale discussed earlier. We are totally responsible for this child at birth. We show our love through our protection. We communicate our love through the senses of touching, feeling, hearing, and tasting.

Although the bonding process is most dramatic at the moment of birth and the first few hours afterward, it continues as the baby grows. Obviously the cutting of the umbilical cord is the most dramatic act of separation, but mothers and fathers report feeling the twinge of letting go at different moments during the first few months of their child's life.

One mother felt it keenly when she went home and left her baby in the hospital nursery for treatment of a minor health problem. Another mother noticed the twinge when she saw her baby turn over for the first time or hold a bottle, small acts of independence accomplished without her. One father distinctly remembers the first time his child smiled at a stranger, displaying the same grin he thought was reserved only for familiar faces. A working mother felt a painful letting-go tug when her maternity leave expired and she had to take her baby to the sitter while she went back to work.

One of the most emotional decisions for a nursing mother is when to wean the baby. Pediatricians tell us one thing; La Leche League tells us another; and our friend down the street gives us a third opinion. I nursed each of our children about six months and then weaned them for a specific reason. Lynn and I would plan an overnight or long weekend away from the children. These plans gave me something to look forward to and minimized the emotional significance of breaking this intimate tie with the baby. Regardless of this plan, weaning our babies was always harder on me than it was on them. This is true of most letting-go emotions.

Decisions about child-rearing philosophies are personal, and we struggle with them. Should we use a pacifier? When should we start disciplining? Can we spoil a four-month-old baby? One source tells us to "answer all their needs; hug and rock them to sleep." Another advises parents to let them cry it out. I was delighted to discover that Derek fell asleep easily by himself if he took a bottle of water to bed but horrified to read that such a bottle could become a "mother substitute." Thankfully I heard one doctor say there are lots of ways to raise a child, and all are okay as long as the child gets a combination of love and structure, firmness and tenderness.

For the baby, birth is the first separation he or she experiences, and experts disagree about the significance of this birth trauma. At about six months, the baby begins to realize he or she is separate from the mother and may feel secure only when the mother is in sight. This is a separation anxiety, and the aim is to build a feeling of security so that the baby gradually feels a sense of security at greater distances and for greater time periods away from the mother. The basic trust established at this point becomes the foundation for autonomy and independence later in life, especially in adolescence.

The baby's physical growth develops in tandem with his or her emotional needs. The tightest physical bonding happens when the baby is cuddly and immobile. As the baby learns to crawl and finally walk, he or she is maturing and learning to feel confident at greater distances from the mother. One therapist even believes it's important that sufficient bonding takes place before the baby learns to walk. If the baby begins to walk too early before he or she bonds tightly, the child may have trouble maintaining a loving, close relationship with the parents in the future.

Should the mother work outside the home during this critically important bonding time? That is never a simple question. For many mothers, the answer is not an option. They work because they need the money.

I stayed home because I was blessed to have the option, and I enjoyed it. I also felt confident that I could do the best job of raising our children at this stage. I often remember the advice of an older mother who stayed home with her young children but works full-time now that her children are in high school.

"I look at it as an investment. I spent time building in them a foundation while they were young. I gave them the consistent love, discipline, and structure they needed, and now I am reaping the rewards of the responsibility and independence they gained. I have the freedom to work and know that they are getting along fine."

TWO-TO-FIVE-YEARS-OLD

As children grow more autonomous and less physically dependent upon their parents, they begin a quest for independence. Born of this time comes the term "terrible twos." Children at this age are beginning to move around quickly, are totally self-centered, have not developed good judgment, and are bent on proving independence at all costs.

This is the age where children continually test the limits; and patterns of obedience formed now have lasting impact. If the rule is the child does not go out the front door alone, that rule must be strictly enforced, with logical, predictable, consistent consequences for disobedience. The principle is "actions bring consequences." Because toddlers are self-centered and interpret the world around them in terms of what's good for them, they learn to repeat behavior that is rewarded and affirmed and avoid behavior that brings unpleasant results.

In spite of strict discipline, we need to acknowledge and allow their quest for independence rather than thwart it, and we need to allow them freedom in the areas where the consequences are acceptable to us. Choice of clothing is a favorite area for toddlers to express their independence. They may be fiercely determined to wear Batman capes over their clothes every day or the layered look of three outfits in one. Generally this is an area where we should let go and compromise, although it is difficult for some parents who enjoy seeing their children in certain outfits.

Starting about age three, hair also becomes an owned decision. I adored our girls in perky wedge cuts, but I'll never forget the day I picked up three-year-old Kendall after preschool. Buckled in the seat next to me, her chubby legs stuck straight out in front of her.

"Nobody likes me," she announced in a grumpy monotone.

"Kendall, whatever makes you think that?" I asked in surprise.

"It's because I don't have long hair," she reasoned, matter-of-factly.

She didn't get her hair cut again for two years.

We must allow our children to start practicing decision making about age two so they begin to sense our confidence in their growing independence and start gaining their own confidence in their ability to do so. We start with simple choices: "Do you want a peanut-butter-and-jelly sandwich or baloney sandwich for lunch?"; "Do you want to wear this blue shirt or this green shirt?" These choices aren't "Do you want to eat lunch?" or "Do you want to get dressed?" The answer no to these questions is unacceptable; those choices are not options. We undermine their confidence in the ability to make decisions if we give them a choice and then tell them they made the wrong decision.

We give them appropriate responsibilities: dumping their wastebaskets, making their beds, and keeping their rooms clean. The less-than-perfect results are acceptable. One mother gave her three-year-old child the responsibility of brushing her teeth. Later the child ended up with lots of cavities because she hadn't brushed correctly. The mother felt bad because she had given her child an inappropriate responsibility.

We teach them good work habits, including the understanding that we all have to do things we don't want to do sometimes. Some things in life are boring or unpleasant, but necessary.

At this age, children are bound to vacillate between fierce independence and clinging dependence. The pendulum of moods can confuse and test a parent's patience. The child who insists upon putting on his own shoes when we're in a hurry to get out the door to a friend's house is the same child who sits on my lap and sucks his thumb when we get to the friend's house instead of joining the other children in the playroom. At home his independence irritated me; now his dependence embarrasses me.

While children make strides toward independence, they constantly need to reaffirm their love and attachment to parents. Children may become clingy when they feel insecure about routines, confused about their parents' coming and going, or pressured by overprotection. Forcing a child to do something at clingy moments only adds to that child's feelings of insecurity. Bernice Weissbourd, who writes a regular column on two-year-olds for *Parents,* describes the confusion of feelings about independence at this age.

> *The tug that your two-year-old feels between independence and dependence may very well match the tug you feel between losing your baby and wanting her to grow up. You may subtly communicate that her baby ways please you, and that you find her willful manner of asserting herself irritating. Without intending to you may then create difficulties for her in this period in which she is motivated to make great strides toward independence.*[1]

Going off to preschool is a milestone of independence, and our children's preschool teacher encouraged parents to be sensitive to separation anxieties that might occur during the first week of school. She asked that one parent be prepared to stay with the child the first couple of days, if the child desired, to ease him or her into the new situation with security.

The first day of preschool I took Kendall. Some children were clingy; others marched right into the room and seemed unaware of their parent's presence in the hallway. Kendall, our youngest at three, walked into the room with an air of importance and announced that I could go home because this was her school. I left, feeling a little cheated because I had planned to spend this first morning with her.

In spite of our children's introduction to school experiences, we remain their most influential and consistent teachers, especially when it comes to their spiritual training. When I began teaching Sunday school classes a few years ago, I learned some valuable tips about what children are capable of understanding at different age levels.

Children's sense of God and their ability to grasp spiritual concepts change significantly as they grow up. For instance, during the preschool years they view God much as they do Santa Claus: unreal and magical. They cannot comprehend the meaning of death and resurrection because death for them is pretend and temporary. It comes from television Westerns. "Bang! Bang! You're dead!"they shout, shooting wooden sticks at each other. "Now let's get up and play something else."

During preschool years, they eagerly devour Bible stories, but some are more appropriate than others. God's creation of the earth, stories about the first family, and stories about Jesus helping people and talking to children give them an understanding of the power of God and of Jesus' love for children. Stories of Issac's sacrifice and the stoning of Stephan demand a maturity they don't have.

Jesus talked of children's accepting response as an example of the faith we all should seek: "I tell you the truth, unless you change and become like little children, you will never enter the kingdom of heaven"(Matt. 18:3).

Children ages two to five have simple, trusting faith, and truth is anything we tell them. They don't reason but they can begin to appreciate the idea of trust in God's promises by comparing Scripture with the reality they know: Night follows day, and spring follows winter just as God promises. We strengthen their budding self-image by teaching them they are children of God and loved by God.

In her book, *Successful Family Devotions*, Mary White— wife, mother, and author—claims that young children are capable of understanding the following basic lessons:

—A concept of God—who He is, His character, His attributes
—Love and respect for the Bible
—Prayer
—Kindness toward others
—Obedience to God and parents
—Knowledge of the common Bible characters

Mrs. White advises parents to use lots of visual aids, physical closeness, repetition, and brevity when teaching their children. At times, a thirty-second prayer may have more impact on a squirmy three-year-old than a five-minute Bible lesson.[2]

The first six years of a child's life are rich with the precious moments and milestones that fill up the pages of the family scrapbooks. Because of the dependency of small children, we are tied to them in a special way that is not duplicated again during their lives. As they march off to elementary school, they begin a new chapter in their lives.

CHAPTER 9

The Middle Years

If we divide childhood into trimesters, this middle trimester probably would be the most delightful period for parents. Children are more self-sufficient, still eager to learn, and still happily and securely tied to the family unit. Like the middle trimester of pregnancy, this is the comfort zone, tucked in between two more tumultuous zones.

This is an age of rapid change and significant growth when children learn to adapt and cooperate to get along with their increasingly important outside world. They begin to spend nights away from home without Mom or Dad. They learn to read, which gives them a sense of control over their lives.

Experts agree that children begin to incorporate something more real into their value systems about age six. This coincides with the period called "latency," in which self-discovery and learning magically unfold for children. This is a time they become less self-centered, and their understanding of right and wrong is not so much based on rewards as the idea of pleasing God or someone else. They are more aware of the world of others. They understand sharing or the meaning of saying, "I'm sorry," not because they are told to share or be sorry but because they want to please someone else. They learn that it's not always easy or pleasurable to do what is right.

They also begin to think more independently and structure their own set of values. Even though we are loosening the reins a bit more now, these six-to-twelve-year-olds still need training and reinforcement as they test their emerging values. They may begin to question some of our concepts and values, as they realize that parents are not always right and as they recognize that people around them live by differing ethical standards. God strengthens us as we answer their questions, relate appropriate Scripture to their real life experiences, and continue to model our faith.

Early elementary school children are adjusting to all-day-long school, new webs of relationships, new adults with new expectations, and many new rules and structures. If they have had the security of structure in the earlier years and learned the importance of obedience, they will try to learn to follow the rules now. Because structure and limits are important to them, the rules must be clearly communicated and understood both at home and at school so that children will feel secure.

The child will also experience some yo-yo-ing between independence and dependence in this stage. Kendall, who sailed through preschool, began to fear going home with friends after school in first grade. She agonized whether or not to accept an invitation and then often cried at recess or called whimpering to come home as soon as she got to the friend's house. Her insecurity puzzled and sometimes irritated me until I thought about what else was going on in her life. Then I understood. Her grandmother had just passed away, and because this was her first experience with death, she was feeling confused and insecure. At school, she was feeling inadequate because she didn't read as well as her best friend. Patience and understanding helped her grow out of these insecurities within a few months, which was according to her timetable, not mine.

Even a ten-year-old sometimes slips back into the total dependency role. Since preschool, I had been "Mom" instead of "Mommy" to Lindsay. For one dramatic, frightening moment, however, on our vacation last summer, I suddenly became "Mommy" again. Lindsay and I were snorkeling together off a craggy beach. Suddenly huge waves came up, and we both crashed into the rocks. "Mommy! Mommy!" I heard her plaintive cries as she looked to me to rescue her. I grabbed her arm between waves, and we crawled among the rocks to shore. We were shaken but safe, and I became "Mom" again.

Giving children responsibility during these years not only increases their independence but also helps their growing sense of confidence, as we recognize and reward their good behavior. We give them privileges and responsibilities because we trust them.

They begin to share more of the duties around the house because they are important members of the family. In addition to making their beds and cleaning their rooms, they can load or unload dishwashers, empty trash cans, fold laundry, and feed their pets. The list of possibilities is endless, but they shouldn't carry an overload of responsibilities. David Elkind in his book *The Hurried Child* warns parents not to overload children with too many responsibilities. This is a temptation in single-parent homes, or homes where both parents work, in which elementary-aged children may be expected to carry a large share of the household duties. If a child is in charge of himself, a younger brother or sister, cleaning up, and dinner preparations every day, all these responsibilities may be too much and cause the child undue stress.

We equip our children during these years by helping them learn to make decisions, set goals and priorities, and think for themselves. We teach them how to be communicative and assertive, yet tactful. The patterns and habits they establish now will likely stay with them through the more challenging, unstable years ahead.

LET THEM MAKE DECISIONS

Our children began making decisions such as what shoes to buy and what activities to join about age six. Obviously they had adult input, but the choices were theirs. Our responsibility was to help them recognize the alternatives and consequences or conditions of each alternative. For example, our daughter might have an option to choose between two pairs of tennis shoes. Color is the biggest difference. I point out that the white ones may get dirty sooner than the navy blue ones, but that's her problem not mine, and she can decide whether to live with that bother. She chooses the white ones. They get scuffed on the way home from the store. I bite my tongue and curb my desire to say "I told you so!" She knows so.

If price is the difference (which it often is), we give our children a different option. Since shoes are a necessity and we pay for necessities at our house, we offer to contribute whatever an average pair of shoes costs. If they choose a more expensive pair, our children pay the difference. That's their choice. We don't tell them how to spend their savings.

One of the ways our children get spending money is through our lunch money arrangement. Hot lunch at their school costs $1.10. We give them $5.50 a week. We also provide the basics: sandwich makings, fruit, carrot and celery sticks, and chips. If they choose to make their own lunch each morning, the money is theirs. They are responsible for posting and checking the school lunch menu, making the decision of whether they want the school lunch, and either getting the money from their envelope or making their lunch. The choices and responsibilities are entirely theirs.

HELP CHILDREN SET GOALS

Setting goals is tied with making decisions and establishing priorities. Several months ago, Lynn attended an all-day seminar about goal setting. He came home with a new sense of direction because he had defined his long- and short-term goals in different areas of his life: spiritual, family, professional, and recreational. He also had identified daily steps that would inch him toward these goals. Kids can benefit from the same practice. First, we have to make goals important to them.

We have a friend who recently dropped out of college because she was not motivated. Unfortunately she doesn't have any future goals or direction at the moment. She is waiting for life to happen rather than making it happen. I hope by the time our children leave home, they will know how to make life happen.

Here are a few general rules for helping children set goals. Be realistic. Help children set goals based on their interests, abilities, and personalities. Although it is important to teach them to deal with both success and failure, we don't want to destine them for failure by continually allowing them to strive for unattainable or unrealistic goals. They need a sprinkling of successful experiences to build confidence. Yet we should encourage them to dream. "Without dreams, you have no goals. Without goals, you have no dreams" goes the old saying.

Children shouldn't set too many goals; the goals should be specific and have time frames; and we should help them celebrate reaching those goals. To get them thinking about goals, we can ask, "Where are you now; where do you want to go; and how are you going to get there?"

One of our children was disappointed with a grade in reading. He set a goal to improve the grade. Because the grade was based on number of books read and reported, he knew he had to read more books during the next semester. He defined a general, attainable goal. Next he needed to define specific steps to reach that goal. Getting an "A" in the class meant reading approximately 1,000 pages. He had twelve weeks left in the grading period so he had to read about eighty-five pages a week or about twelve pages a day. Then he needed a plan. He decided he would read before bed, but we knew and he knew that he always falls asleep when he reads in bed. Instead we suggested reading before dinner each night. He agreed. With that plan, he broke his long-range goal down into weekly and daily goals.

Another of our children set a goal to swim in the city swim meet. It was a borderline, attainable goal, since we live in a community of more than 100,000 people, and only the best six girls and boys swim in each event in the city meet. We knew competition would be tough, so we helped her decide her favorite and best stroke and then encouraged her to work hardest on that one. She knew that in her free time during practice she should concentrate on that stroke.

In spite of her efforts, she missed qualifying for the city meet by two-hundredths of a second. She missed her goal by a hair but she enjoyed participating; she improved her skills; she learned something about perseverance and determination; and she learned to handle failure and frustration.

As parents, we model goal setting and follow through as we stick to a diet, a regular exercise program, or daily Bible study. We need to share our goals, successes, and failures with our children, so they know we all live through struggles with a combination of victories and defeats. We also set common goals as a family and share ideas of how to reach those goals. We try to cut our public service bill by turning off lights and turning down the heat. We try to watch less television and read more by declaring a "No TV Day" each week, by limiting our watching to an hour a day, and by reading together one night a week as a family.

When Lynn turned thirty-nine years old, the kids and I decided to give him his fortieth birthday present a year early. Since he likes to travel, we made up an itinerary for a special family vacation, going to places he'd always wanted to visit. We made a scrapbook of ways we would save money for the trip over the next year: Derek at eleven promised to save aluminum cans; Lindsay at nine donated a portion of her weekly allowance; and Kendall at five gave up chewing gum. We had a garage sale; we cut back on Christmas and birthday presents; and we put all our loose change in a coffee can decorated with pictures and "Send Lynn on a Vacation." As a family, we set a goal, defined steps to reach it, and worked together to attain it. We all kept our promises and the vacation that took a year to make, was the best we've ever had.

SPIRITUAL GROWTH

This middle trimester is a period of tremendous spiritual growth for children as they begin to think more conceptually and move away from the fantasy concept of God. They understand such doctrines as salvation, grace, God, and Satan, and are more able to accept that God doesn't always answer their prayers exactly as they ask. Sometimes God says

"No" or "Wait" because God gives us what we need, not necessarily what we want. Children learn we don't always get instant gratification.

During this period, a child may begin to tithe. Our church believes that children at age eight may be able to make a commitment to pledge a certain amount of money each week to the church. But they emphasize, that decision is up to the parents and child.

We began giving our children allowances at age five with the instruction that some money was to save, some to spend, and some for God. They were responsible for taking a portion out each week before Sunday school. We didn't nag or scold. Sometimes it was forgotten; sometimes they took extra. We do the same thing.

This may be the time children choose to make a personal commitment to the Lord. A fifth grader in a recent children's worship service at our church told how she asked the Lord into her heart:

> *For a long time, I thought I was born a Christian because my parents were Christians. Then I learned that I had to ask Jesus into my heart myself. That didn't sound too hard. So one night before bed when I was six years old, I asked Jesus into my heart. Both my parents were with me, and we prayed together, and then I went to sleep. When I woke up, I didn't feel any different, and I didn't notice that anything in my life changed.*
>
> *It wasn't until this year that I began to realize I could pray and talk to Jesus all by myself, every morning and all during the day. I could pray for thirty seconds or five minutes, anytime, anywhere. That's when I began to understand the meaning of a personal relationship with the Lord.*

Obviously there is no one appropriate age for a child to make a personal commitment to receive Christ into his or her life. It may be preschool or first grade. Some people question whether a child so young can accept Jesus and believe because such a choice demands maturity and understanding. Larry Christenson in *The Christian Family* disagrees. "His (the child's) problem is not a lack of faith but a lack of experience," he explains. "The job of the parent is to let that faith become a doorway to experience."[1]

Parents need to tell their children how to make a commitment to the Lord, but we must assure them that this is a personal choice and we will not pressure them. We can lead, but we can't get them there. How do we lead?

We lead by slowly building a firm foundation in the Lord. As children mature and show more understanding, Mary White suggests reading John 3:1–21 and Isaiah 53 with them and sharing the Four Spiritual Laws: (1) God loves you and offers a wonderful plan for your life. (2) Man is sinful and separated from God. Therefore, he cannot know and experience God's love and plan for his life. (3) Jesus Christ is God's only provision for man's sin. Through Him you can know and experience God's love and plan for your life. (4) We must individually receive Jesus Christ as Savior and Lord; then we can know and experience God's love and plan for our lives. Ideally, this knowledge is shared over a period of time.[2]

Our own twelve-year-old son, on the brink of adolescence and tugged by peer influence, sometimes questions the commitment of his Christianity. "But I want to have fun," he wails.

Don't Christians have fun? I wonder. Do we look and act happy and full of life? Where does he get a scolding, scowling, finger-shaking, holier-than-thou image of a Christian? How are we modeling our relationship with the Lord? At this age, our children watch us carefully and hold us accountable.

As they teeter on the brink of adolescence at the end of this age period, we're conscious of their changing bodies and minds. As we watch them mature, we may feel that familiar painful twinge of regret. I watch chubby hands with dimpled knuckles become strong and capable. I watch compact, squatty bodies stretch out to lean lengths. I notice they are spending more time in their rooms and less time lingering over dinner. They like the mirror, telephone, clothes, and radios better, and my pancakes less.

Life is tugging at their sleeves.

CHAPTER 10

Adolescence

"God made babies so precious and adorable that we don't mind getting up at 3:00 A.M. to feed them . . . and He made adolescents so obnoxious that we don't mind when they leave home. . . ."

Hearing that little ditty two years ago when our oldest was a delightful ten-year-old, I laughed heartily. Now as he approaches thirteen and displays most of the characteristics of adolescence, I have a far different appreciation for the truth in that humor.

I look back on my own adolescence as an unstable time of life. Peer pressure was painfully powerful, but my peers were as confused as I was. I was torn between loving and hating my parents. I spent a lot of time worrying about who I was, where I was going, and what I wanted to do when I got there.

Adolescence is a tough time. For kids, it's an in-between age, a transition between childhood and adulthood when they don't have the privileges and excuses of being children nor the total freedom and maturity of being adults.

It is a time of struggle for autonomy and independence, much like the struggle a two-year-old faces in trying to separate from his or her parents. "An adolescent is a two-year-old with hormones and wheels," describes child psychiatrist Foster Cline, who sees many similarities between these two age groups.

For parents, adolescence is the rubber-meets-the-road time when we gradually loosen the reins and allow our children to test their wings. It is a time we consciously change the way we show our love for them, as we command less and trust more.

For both kids and parents, it is an emotionally trying time. "Separation is a mutual experience for adolescent and parent—both have to deal with the ambivalences and rewards of letting go," writes Michael V. Bloom in *Adolescent Parental Separation.*[1]

Some parents seem to weather the adolescent years better than others. "They were rich, rewarding, challenging years," said one enthusiastic parent who is on the other side of the experience. "I thoroughly enjoyed our children as teenagers!"

Another disagrees. "It was one fight after another. My teenagers were moody, selfish, and impossible to live with."

What's the difference? Probably it's not so much a difference in the teenagers as in the parents. Three distinct qualities seem to affect a parent's ability to cope during adolescence: attitude, understanding, and expectations.

ATTITUDE

"This may shock you," writes Charles Swindoll, "but I believe the single most significant decision I make on a day-to-day basis is my choice of attitude." This quote from his book *Strengthening Your Grip* is posted on our refrigerator door because it helps me when I face circumstances I can't change. My children's adolescence is one of those circumstances. They are on a journey to maturity. To get there, they have to go through adolescence with all its up-and-down moods and dramatic rebellions, which I can't change or control. But I can change and control my attitude.

As parents, we can approach our children's adolescence optimistically with a willingness to listen, compromise, and choose an attitude of pragmatic determination: Given the task at hand, let's make the most of this period. Or we can view the entire period as a stormy season to be endured, as we unbendingly brace ourselves against the inevitable conflicts. The point is we have power in the attitude we choose.

UNDERSTANDING

Our understanding is our willingness to walk in our children's shoes and recognize their needs. Do we remember what it felt like to have an unpredictable squeaky voice or a pizza face (as I overheard one teenager's description of another's acne problem)? How do we feel now when we have an obvious blemish or a bad haircut? We feel self-conscious.

How do we feel when we hear of a gathering of our friends that didn't include us? We feel left out. How do we feel when everyone else around us in the exercise class can do one hundred crisp situps, but we can't get past thirty-five? We feel peer pressure. How do we react when our teenager questions the way we dress, act, or think? In spite of our surface defensiveness, I'll bet deep down we all feel a little insecure.

Adolescents feel the same emotions we do only more intensely because they aren't as sure of themselves as we are. Because of their immaturity, they are less rooted, since maturity brings more confident grounding. We need to be sensitive to their need to separate from us but still be affirmed by us. In an attempt to better understand what they face and feel every day, we need to listen, not judge, and try to emphasize, not criticize.

EXPECTATIONS

Our hopes become our expectations, and those expectations are realistic or unrealistic based on our knowledge and experience. The more we know or remember about adolescence, the more realistic our expectations will be about the tranquility of life in our homes during these years.

Adolescence is the transformation from dependence on parents to mature independence. The adolescents' need to separate from parents is real. We can accept and facilitate this need, easing the process or we can thwart their efforts, making the process more traumatic. Even the Lord speaks out in Isaiah: "I reared children and brought them up, but they have rebelled against me" (Isa. 1:2).

Rebellion is a normal part of the separation process as adolescents define what they think apart from what we think.

They are continuing to test, formulate, and build value systems of their own, but the construction often hammers away at parents' values. They may reject what we think, but we shouldn't interpret that as a personal rejection. They are not rejecting us. In his book *Too Big to Spank*, Jay Kesler writes about adolescents, "To be young is to question and test. It doesn't mean they are hostile. It doesn't mean that they are going to leave the time-tested things permanently."[2]

If we don't allow our adolescents to develop their own individuality, they have one of two choices: to rebel dramatically or comply quietly. Neither is desirable. The dramatic rebellion may mean running away from home as we've already discussed. On the other hand the compliant child may face problems later in life.

A thirty-five-year-old Christian woman told me how her mother used to march her off to the hairdresser every six months until she was twenty-one years old for the same short bob and frizzy permanent. She detested the style and ritual, but it never occurred to her to resist her mother's control over her life. After graduating from college and moving away from home, she still struggled with her lack of self-confidence that had paralyzed her in adolescence.

"I didn't go through those normal adolescent rebellions until after I was married, and then it was painfully difficult to separate from my parents, think of myself as an individual, and gain confidence in myself." She paused, then continued; "This may sound silly, but I hope my daughter experiences some rebellion in her teenage years because I know such feelings are healthy—necessary."

The mother of this now thirty-five-year-old woman had the expectation that adolescence meant the same smooth sailing, the same control and obedience as the earlier years of childhood. "In all fairness to my mother, she loved me and had no idea what she was doing to me by controlling me in that way," the daughter said.

According to researchers who study adolescent behavior, adolescents strive for three forms of autonomy in seeking independence: behavioral, emotional, and value autonomy. Behavioral autonomy results in conflicts about dating, recreational activities, choice of friends, curfews, clothes, and money.

Emotional autonomy means self-reliance, self-control, and the transfer of emotional attachment from family members to peers. Close friends are extremely important to adolescents. They begin to spend more time on the telephone and less time at home. They may form friendships with other adults: a coach, teacher, or neighbor, to fill the spaces of separateness they are building in their relationship with their parents. Parents should see this as a positive step not a personal rejection.

Value autonomy is the adolescent's struggle to define and claim moral and religious values, vocational choices, and life goals. It is a search for self-identity and clarification. Seeking value autonomy often results in the rebellion we've discussed, and the questioning and rejecting of parental rules and values that causes emotional confrontations.[3]

As adolescents seek their autonomy and pull away from us both physically and emotionally, we need to understand that their needs differ from our needs. "Letting go is the key to peaceful and meaningful coexistence between parents and teenagers: as parents, our need is to be needed; as teenagers, their need is not to need us. To let go when we want to hold on requires the utmost generosity and love," writes Haim Ginott in *Between Parent and Teenager*.[4]

Adolescents also need the stability and reassuring warmth of our love even as they tug away. One counselor urges parents to fill their teenagers' emotional tanks whenever they zoom in for a pit stop on "low" or "empty."They still need hugs, back rubs, and eye-to-eye conversations even if the opportunities for sharing are fewer.

As we journey through the adolescent years with our children, we benefit from reviewing our goals periodically. We want to give our children a firm foundation of Christian principles, a healthy ability to accept and give love, and a sense of family. We want them to think for themselves, become problem solvers, and learn to accept responsibilities. As parents, we decide the issues on which we will stand firm; we encourage, not discourage their growing independence;

and we loosen the reins as they grow. According to our mathematical concept of 100 percent dependence at birth and 100 percent independence at maturity, our teenagers are nearing the 75 percent mark as they enter junior high. Where are our reins?

JUNIOR HIGH YEARS

Junior high students show distinct signs of maturing and separating. They may grow moody and seek more privacy in their bedrooms that they decorate to reflect their personalities. Posters and radios or stereos are common pieces of the bedroom decor. Many beg for and receive telephone extensions. They retreat, either to their rooms, behind earphones, or to friends' houses. They vacillate between dependence and independence like a playful puppy wanting attention one minute and a growling dog the next.

The junior high years bring so many major changes in the life of a teenager that many experts identify this time as a child's most difficult period. "Junior high probably is the most stressful time in a child's life," claims behavioral researcher and father of six Del Elliott, who has made a nationwide survey of adolescents. "Between the ages of 11 and 15, kids experience tremendous changes. Their bodies change, peers begin to compete effectively with parents for influence, and their concepts of right and wrong are changing."

If a child goes from an elementary school to a junior high between sixth and seventh grade, the structure of the system means major changes. Usually the school is in a different building with different schedules that require decisions about courses and extracurricular activities. Instead of one teacher, the child faces seven teachers in seven different subjects. The thirteen-year-old has to decide between computers or Spanish, whereas before he or she had no curriculum decisions. Instead of enjoying all sports, now he or she must narrow the options, perhaps giving up tennis to be on the soccer team. Focus becomes more specific and choices more important as a child suddenly is forced to think about a future. Setting goals seems critical.

Because of their increased autonomy, junior high students have more freedom to make choices and face more pressures and temptations than they did in elementary school. Sex, alcohol, and drugs are issues they will confront.

In speaking to parents, a national expert on teenage drug use warns, "The biggest mistake parents make is believing their children will never use drugs." Statistics show that nationally almost half of all junior high students start drugs between the ages of thirteen and fifteen, and more than half start their drinking experience before high school.

The consequences of their actions become more frightening as they grow up, but this doesn't mean we tighten instead of loosen the reins. We continue to love, teach, discipline, and model, and let them go with faith and prayers. If they make mistakes, we turn those errors into opportunities for learning.

Because of peer pressure, parents may notice marked behavior changes in their junior high students. For instance, a girl who has been a model child may suddenly begin dressing in a bizarre manner—punk instead of preppy or sloppy instead of clean cut. Through her appearance, she is trying to make a statement to her friends more than to her family. An adolescent who appears to maintain a strong attachment to his or her parents may be labeled a "goody goody" by the peer group. So the new look is not a rejection of parental values but an attempt to change an image at school.

If this manner of dress becomes a source of conflict at home, parents should put the problem in perspective and view this as a chance to adjust their attitudes to a relatively harmless change in their child. According to Elliott, who also teaches parenting seminars,

> *Starting in junior high, parents need to decide in which areas they will compromise, and which areas they will stand firm.*
>
> *For instance, we've decided on matters of style and taste we will compromise. That includes dress, hair, music, and cleanliness of their rooms. On matters of value, we will not yield. That includes telling the truth and showing respect for others, which means they*

tell us where they are going and when they will return. As they reached junior high, we gave our children more autonomy in matters of style, but we didn't budge on values.[5]

SENIOR HIGH SCHOOL

If adolescents are "two-year-olds with hormones and wheels," they come of age in senior high school. For teenagers, cars are the wheels to freedom. For parents, they are the means to coronaries. A teen behind the wheel brings on a whole new world of worries and responsibilities. Many of the worries are well-founded. Most of us know teenagers who were killed or injured in car accidents. Even if we trust our teenager's driving, we worry about the other crazy drivers on the road.

Adolescents are now making decisions that have greater consequences than the decisions of earlier years. Not only do they decide when to pull out into traffic or how fast to go, but they also decide where to go and when to come home. Many parents put restrictions on car use. For instance, the teenagers must keep a certain grade point average, contribute to the cost of the insurance, upkeep, and gasoline (if it is a family car), and inform parents where they are going and when they will be back. "I don't want to worry and I do want to know who will be home at 6:00 P.M. for dinner," one mother explains simply.

In other words, the use of the car is a contractual agreement. Breaking a rule means a broken contract that results in the loss of a privilege: no car for a specific period of time. There needs to be no argument or nagging. We don't discipline them as we did when they were nine years old. We recognize their ability to reason and we follow through with the consequences as they were defined. We are consistent and fair. We don't provoke them to anger by enforcing a punishment that does not fit the infraction.

What is our role in their decision-making process? More and more, our role becomes advisory. Our goal is to teach them how to think not what to think, so we contribute thoughts and ideas as we help them explore options and consequences. Unless those consequences are life threatening or morally threatening, they own the decisions.

I know a father who interfered with his daughter's decision to go out for cheerleading because he saw it as morally threatening to her. He remembers it as a difficult moment in parenting.

Their older daughter had been a cheerleader in the same large public high school. The parents agonized through the experience with her, watching her struggle with the pressure of the role, the popularity image, the strain on her values, the web of relationships woven around the cheerleader role, and the time it took away from her studies. "It was a negative experience for her," her father said. When their second daugher reached the age to try out for cheerleading, they said it was not an option for her just then. They knew this child could not cope with the pressures of the experience at her level of maturity.

Another family had a son Eric, attending the same high school. He was a gifted football player who was recruited by major colleges across the country and the University of Colorado in his hometown. His choice of college was a major decision, not life-threatening or morality-threatening, but maybe life-altering. His parents felt strongly about the outcome and offered their advice.

"We thought he should take the opportunity to go out of state because it was time to cut the cord and enter a new phase of life. But we assured him the decision was his," his father said.

Pressure increased as this high school senior traveled all over the country visiting schools. On the last night before he had to make a decision, Michigan coach Bo Schembechler sat in Eric's living room, sipping soft drinks and talking about the opportunities for him in Michigan.

Eric decided to spend that night alone at his father's dental office where he could think and pray about his decision. As he left home, his father again assured him the choice was his and whatever he chose, they would support him. At the end of a sleepless night, he decided to attend the University of Colorado. His parents accepted and supported his decision.

The more we encourage our growing children to think

for themselves, the more they care about what we think. They feel safe listening to our opinions if they know we won't force those opinions on them.

Sometimes children resist making decisions. A mother complained that her fifteen-year-old daughter refused to make any decisions, such as whether to go to a party, what to wear to school, or what to order at a restaurant. "How can I get across to her that she is old enough to handle these decisions on her own?"

When children need help gaining confidence in their ability to make decisions or assume responsibilities, limit their options. I feel overwhelmed with options when I walk into a wallpaper store. I need someone to narrow my choices by handing me two appropriate books and saying "Choose from these." We can play the same role with our adolescents as we guide them by limiting their choices when they seem to lack confidence in making decisions. For example, we can help them explore reasons why they might be hesitant to attend a party. We discuss their fears with them and focus again on their options.

What if a teenager buckles to the pressures of high school? What if parents find their adolescent is involved with drugs or alcohol or engaged in unacceptable behavior and they feel they have no control?

I talked to a single Christian mother in this situation. She had been full circle with three teenagers and had faced every imaginable problem. She felt at the end of her coping rope when she discovered a national support group called "Toughlove," in this case based on the premise that if we love our children, we must make them responsible for their actions.

> *I was one of those mothers who thought it was too late: I'd done everything wrong when they were little. I was too permissive; I overlooked what they did because I felt sorry for their growing up without a father. This group made me realize that if I loved them, I had to teach them to be responsible for their actions and to expect to suffer consequences.*

That was not easy. At age sixteen her son began drinking. Time and time again, he came home drunk and passed out on the living room floor. Eventually he ran up debts, lost his driver's license, and even stole cars.

Through Toughlove, this mother realized she had to take care of herself and teach her son to take care of himself. She realized her bottom line was "I will not allow a drunk in my house." That gave her son a choice. If he wanted to live at home, he had to stay sober. She would get him help and support him, but she would not allow a drunk in her house. If he came home drunk, he had to leave.

> *It tore my heart out but it was the only solution to our problems, and it worked. He's twenty-one years old now, he's sober, and he's paying back all his debts. Not a day goes by that he doesn't tell me he loves me and thanks me for caring enough to be tough and help him become the person he is.*

What about the spiritual life of our teenagers? What should Christian parents be doing during adolescence to be sure our teenagers are growing "in the grace and knowledge of the Lord and Savior Jesus Christ" (2 Peter 3:18)?

Ideally we would like our children to be active in church youth groups, sing in the choir, take leadership positions in church activities, and enthusiastically enjoy all of it. Let's face it, however; that doesn't always happen. Many teenagers begin to question, reject, or even rebel against the values of the Christian faith, and parents feel helpless.

The questioning in this area of their lives is no different from the questioning in other areas. It's part of the normal separation and maturing process. As children, they accumulated Scripture and parroted it back to us. Now they are trying to assimilate that knowledge and do something with what they have learned. And their questioning is not all bad.

First of all, most experts agree that if a child has received a foundation of spiritual training, that core of beliefs will guide the child through the storms of adolescence, and he or she will return to those values no matter what detours are taken. Secondly, at a Sunday school training session, I learned that we have to question our faith to own it. We internalize our faith through our questions. As we struggle, we grow and reach a deeper level of commitment that unquestioning people never reach.

"Why are churches losing adolescents?" distraught parents ask. If you ask the kids, they claim, "It's boring." or "Christians don't have fun." They express some vague responses that indicate they aren't comfortable at church or they don't find it relevant to their lives at the moment.

Recently I heard a doctor claim, on a Christian talk show, that we need to deal more honestly with adolescents' sexual energy. The minimum message we must communicate is that their feelings are okay; it's ungodly sexual literature that's not.

As Christians, we need to help our teenagers appreciate their sexuality and view it as the gift God meant it to be, while acknowledging their frustration and energy. "Celebrate puberty with each child," advises a counselor. "Welcome them into adulthood. Explain to them they now have a beautiful right and tremendous responsibility in their bodies. Help them take pride in that responsibility."

This is the age to begin talking about the importance of choosing a marriage partner. The divorce statistics show that people are not adequately prepared for marriage or have unrealistic expectations about the person they choose. The ministers of our church no longer marry couples without premarital counseling, and they plead with parents to begin earlier to emphasize the importance of choosing the right partner.

Should parents force their teenagers to attend church? One father insisted his children be involved in some spiritual training at least once a week, but he gave them more options. For instance if his children were involved in Young Life, they might miss Sunday school. This family supplemented their church attendance with a regular Sunday night Bible study, when they would discuss Scripture, share prayer requests, and pray together.

Dr. James Dobson believes it is appropriate for parents to require all teenagers to attend church with the family because "I have promised the Lord that we will honor him in this home, and that includes remembering the Sabbath to keep it holy."[6]

As our adolescents near high school graduation, they should be totally on their own, though living at home. I know one family who gives their high school seniors almost total responsibility for their lives. For years, they have had part-time jobs. They do their own laundry, budget their money, set their own curfews, and make some family meals. "After all," the mother explains, "within a few months they will be doing all this on their own. And we want them to be ready."

Whether or not we feel they are ready or not has much to do with our emotional reaction to their leaving home. One mother who still made the bed daily for her eighteen-year-old son was terribly depressed at the thought of his leaving home. Another mother clarified the source of that feeling, "Last year when our son was a junior in high school, I was depressed at the thought of his going off to college. He seemed so unprepared. But this year, I see him making good decisions and showing such maturity that I'm really excited for him. I know he's ready to go."

When we know we've completed a job, we have the freedom to give it up. If I make a cake for a friend's birthday, I am not going to feel good about carrying that cake out the door until it is frosted and decorated. I would not want to give it to her half-baked. My husband is a lawyer. He feels frustrated if a deadline nears and he is not pleased with his brief. He doesn't feel it is done. If we finish our job as parents and prepare our children to face the world, we let go of them more easily and contentedly.

CHAPTER 11

Parental Preparation

"In this world nothing is sure but death and taxes," wrote Benjamin Franklin hundreds of years ago. For parents, there is a third sure thing: our children will grow up and leave home—eventually.

It's part of God's plan for families and predictable in our future. Parenting is a temporary job description; our role has planned obsolescence. Years ago I saw a circle graph that represented a person's lifespan. I was amazed at the small wedge designating the child-rearing years. It seemed surprisingly skinny in comparison with the rest of the circle. Those of us immersed in this wedge forget there are other wedges beyond this. Yet just around the circle a smidgen, the inevitable empty nest awaits us. How we adapt to life in that wedge has much to do with how we prepare for it now while our children are growing up.

I heed the words of H. Norman Wright in *Seasons of a Marriage:*

> *When all the children leave home and the nest is empty, some parents have no idea who they are or what to do with themselves. Their identity, both as individuals and as family members, has been so tied up in mothering and fathering that they are lost. They feel worthless and useless. They feel robbed of their roles and their children.[1]*

That's a warning. We web our lives so intricately into the lives of our children that we can't move forward. We get all tangled up in our own apron strings. The process happens so subtly, so slowly, yet so completely through the years we don't even realize what's happened until we find ourselves teetering on the brink of the next era, totally unprepared for life without children.

Many years ago, I became determined to reach the childless era with a sense of purpose instead of despair and confusion. Unwittingly my mother motivated my determination. She kept telling me these child-rearing years were the best years of my life. She implied it was all downhill after the children left home. I'm not trying to prove her wrong; I'm only trying to prove the value of preparation.

All of life is a series of changes. God never leaves us in one place too long. We walk through a rhythmic pattern of peaks and valleys, broken periodically by places of peaceful stability. We face crises and changes. We rejoice in our challenges; we grow and adjust. In spite of some stumbles, we move ahead with faith. As I look back over the past eras of my life, childhood flows together as one era; adolescence as another; then college; most importantly, marriage; and finally childbearing.

I entered marriage with little preparation and motherhood with even less. Although the years have been rich and rewarding, my adjustments were not smooth. My first few years in each era were rocky.

Before our wedding, Lynn and I went through the required premarital counseling. Our minister was tolerantly patient with our nonchalant attitude about this ritual, which at the time was just another item on our prewedding "to do" list. We had no problems and we anticipated none. We were filled with blissful and romantic notions of our happily-ever-after life together.

The minister obviously read our thoughts as he opened our first session. "You are a wonderful couple," he began slowly, "but neither of you is perfect. You have faults, and you are bound to irritate each other and have disagreements in the years to come. In fact," he continued, "as exciting as a wedding is, I wouldn't trade places with you for anything. My wife and I had some difficult times adjusting to marriage, and both of us agree our relationship today is much better than when we walked down the aisle fifteen years ago."

I listened with a sense of smugness. We, I sniffed, will be different. We, I now concede, were no different. I faced the same rocky adjustment to parenthood. If anything, it was more difficult. In marriage there were spaces of separateness. In motherhood there were none. Suddenly as if overnight, I found myself totally responsible for this noodle-necked infant who couldn't do anything for himself. Certainly I was inexperienced and ill-suited.

I recently read with interest how some high schools today are trying to give students a preview of parenting. Each student receives an egg to care for. Students must not let their eggs out of their sight unless they arrange for an egg-sitter. Always at the end of the week, the students are overwhelmed with the constant responsibility of parenting.

So was I. Yet through the 3:00 A.M. feedings, the colicky crying, and nonstop caring, our love grows as we weave the fibers of our lives together. In fact, the total dependency, which is so overwhelming, is also the endearing quality that breeds the bonding.

Within a family, these years of total dependency pass quickly. We had three babies in five years, and during that time I felt like a character in a Charlie Chaplin movie, frantically racing nonstop through the days, trying to meet the needs of the one demanding the loudest.

I was certain life would never be any different, yet the years disappeared. And when Lynn and I made the decision we would have no more children at the end of that period, I slipped into a terrible depression. Even though I knew it was the right decision for us, I felt as if a precious purpose of my life was over. Parts of my body had fulfilled and completed their God-given function. My uterus would never again feel life stirring; my breasts would never again produce milk. Since childhood, I was aware that God was preparing my body to bloom with life. Now I'd reached a peak. This was the first step downward.

I have outgrown those nostalgic feelings. Our youngest now is in elementary school, and I'm happy where God has put me in life. I'm still so maternal that I grab and nuzzle babies whenever I can, but I'm thankful for the changes our children's growing independence gives our family. Going to the grocery store used to be the major accomplishment of my day. Now I can squeeze in a week's shopping in less than an hour on the way home from an evening meeting. I have more hours to read, write, take Bible study classes, and nurture other relationships.

Time passes, and children grow out of their dependency as quickly as they grow out of their Dr. Dentons, high chairs, and swing sets. Year by year, as they inch their way to maturity, they give us more freedom and more chunks of time to ourselves. The process of gaining independence is mutual. And it should be.

"The parent must gain his freedom from the child so that the child can gain his freedom from the parent," write Marguerite and Willard Beecher in *Parents on the Run.*[2] Letting go, then, involves two goals: weaning the child from the parents, and weaning the parents from the child. We prepare them for life without us as we prepare ourselves for life without them.

We've discussed the ways we wean children from parents. Let's consider some ways we wean ourselves from our children. Many of the principles are the same, only applied in reverse.

SENSE OF SELF

Take the sense of self, for example. This is the recognition that we are separate from our children. We have to separate our needs from their needs, our egos from their egos, and our emotions from their emotions. It sounds like a simple notion, but it is an area where we get subtly tangled in a web of interdependence. Sometimes while meeting our children's needs, we lose our sense of self.

As Christians, we are raised on the idea of selflessness. Sometimes especially as a mother, I've carried that idea too far and become so selfless that I had no sense of self-worth left. Perhaps laying down my life for others means giving up some of my wants and conveniences but not all my needs.

I need time alone with God, time alone with my husband, and exercise. I need all three every day. Our children know I have these needs, and if they see me constantly sacrificing these needs to meet their wants, they suffer too. They begin to sense that I'm not taking care of myself and mimic that behavior. If parents model the fact that we take care of ourselves, our children learn to take care of themselves.

If we sacrifice our values to meet our children's needs, we also lose our sense of self that is reflected in the consistency of our discipline. If I believe my values are important, I don't compromise those values to make our children happy or minimize a conflict.

I know a single mother who learned long ago to compromise in an effort to keep peace around her house. She didn't stand up for what she believed to be right and wrong. Time and time again she compromised with her two children to avoid disagreements. Before long she lost the definition of her values, and her sense of self became swallowed up by her children's demands. Dying to self doesn't mean compromising our God-given values and standards. We have to stand up for and defend those values, sometimes confronting others, especially our children.

We need to separate our egos from their egos. One mother in our neighborhood is tied to her daughter's weight problem. Her daughter is only a few pounds overweight, but this mother fears that her daughter's appearance is a reflection on her. She nags and bribes her daughter to lose weight. Although the weight problem undoubtedly is important to the girl, her mother is handling the touchy subject as if it were more important to her than her daughter.

I know a father whose ego got tangled up with his son's progress in school. The teachers recommended that the boy repeat kindergarten to gain more maturity for first grade. The father refused the advice and pushed his son ahead to the detriment of the child.

We need to be sure our ego needs are not dependent

upon our children. If our children are our greatest achieve-
ment, we should seek new interests. Women seem more
vulnerable to this than men. Joyce Landorf in *Changepoints*
writes, "If a woman rigidly restricts herself, her mind, her
creative talents, and her sole attention to children—placing
their needs and wants above her husband's or even her own
desires—she is in for a dreadful time during the season of
empty nests."[3]

Separating our emotions from our children's emotions is
difficult. Their moods become our moods; their grief, our
grief. We need to separate ourselves from their ups and downs
and not be controlled by their moods. It's not always easy.

I called a friend the other morning to take care of some
church business. Her "hello" gave her away. She'd had a bad
morning. It was her fifth-grade daughter Lisa, a beautiful,
strong-willed child on the brink of adolescence. "She was in a
terrible mood" my friend sighed, sounding drained and
frustrated. "She pulled the silent treatment on me, eating
breakfast without a word and leaving for school without
saying goodbye. I'm so depressed. I feel just like I did when
she was two years old, and her mood could ruin my day."

We have to distinguish between their problems and our
problems and not paralyze ourselves with guilt. Too often, we
play the blame game and allow ourselves to come out guilty.
He has a cold because I didn't remind him to take a coat. She
doesn't get her homework done because she watches me
procrastinate. They are bored and irritable because I won't
take them to the movies.

NURTURE OUR SENSE OF SELF

We nurture our sense of self by spending time alone,
which gives us a chance to refill our cups and recharge our
batteries, even as Jesus did. Some people seek more alone
time than others. I know men who regularly spend hours or
days alone fishing. Other people hike or jog. I have a friend, a
family counselor, who deals daily with other peoples' personal problems and then faces the usual challenges at home
as a husband and father. His secret for coping, he told me, is
taking an entire day or a weekend off alone several times a

year, totally away from his everyday distractions, to sort through his priorities and redefine his goals.

My alone time always seems limited. It consists of a precious twenty minutes early in the morning before the children get up, or it occurs coincidentally in the middle of something else: a half hour waiting in the car during a child's piano lesson; a morning or afternoon at home where the phone, the buzzer on the dryer, or dust on the furniture interrupts and distracts. Sometimes I seek more timeless solitude. Recently I asked my family for the special birthday gift of time alone, a whole glorious day off in the mountains from sunup to sundown: a day for myself to pray, think, read, listen to God, and redefine my goals as I explored that nebulous question "Who am I?"

My definition of myself seems to hinge on what I am doing and what I want to do. Some questions that stimulated my goal setting were these: What do I like to do? What don't I like to do? What makes me happy? What angers me? What would I like to do before I die—as a person, wife, and mother—physically, professionally, and spiritually? Where does God want me to use my energies? And how can I minister to others?

In her book *Gift from the Sea*, Anne Morrow Lindbergh writes about spending time alone to gain perspective on her life and her relationships. The solitude was essential, and the seashore offered her analogies. "As the sea tossed up its gifts, shells rare and perfect—so the mind left to its ponderings, brings up its own treasures of the deep."[4]

Rarely do we let our minds ponder for hours. Usually our thoughts are cluttered by the countless details that rule our lives and demand our attention. Yet when we are alone, we quickly get through that cluttered layer down into the next level of more meaningful thoughts where the treasures exist. Time alone gives us an opportunity to redefine our sense of self.

NURTURE OTHER RELATIONSHIPS

In addition to nurturing our sense of self, we wean ourselves from our children by nurturing other relationships and other interests in our lives. We start by focusing on our God-given priorities. If we keep God's order, the first relationship we faithfully nurture is our relationship with our heavenly Father. He should be first in our lives, and if we are in prayer and in the Word, we receive the guiding strength of the Holy Spirit.

As I have said before, I need quiet time alone with the Lord each day, and I get it most days because it is a priority. My day goes best when I seek that time early in the morning before the children are up. I require the blessings of strength and peace to get through that tornado hour when each member of the family needs help to leave the house on time. I pray each morning for the fruits of the Spirit, and I usually need every one of them.

My time with the Lord is my energizing time. I am a machine but I am worthless without the electricity, which makes the machine work. God is my power source, and I need to plug into Him every morning to get the power to make it through the day.

I don't think God is angry with me when I don't get the quiet time. It's just that I don't receive the blessings that quiet time brings me. Through the Word, I gain knowledge of God's promises and God's will for my life. Through prayer, I claim those promises. I talk to God and listen to Him. He is the organizer of my life. He is my first priority and He keeps all my other priorities in order.

Bible studies, small groups, and prayer chains also help me feel connected to the Lord. Bible studies discipline me to learn the Word. Small groups hold me accountable to the growth I seek, and prayer chains help me feel a part of the body of believers. These are the pieces of my spiritual life that keep me close to my heavenly Father.

According to God's order, the next relationship we nurture is the marriage relationship. If we are blessed with a spouse, God tells us the marriage relationship takes priority over the parent-child relationship. "A man leaves his father and mother and cleaves to his wife, and they become one flesh" (Gen. 2:24 RSV). But children easily become the cement that holds that flesh together as parents grow apart during the hectic, child-rearing years.

Children can steal the life out of a marriage so stealthily that parents don't even notice they are strangers until they find themselves alone at dinner with nothing to talk about but the children. It's no wonder. By the time we diaper, burp, feed, soothe, and bathe our infants, and chauffeur, feed, encourage, counsel, and tutor our older children, there is precious little left over to devote to the marriage relationship.

Although countless books are written on how to improve the marriage relationship, one simple rule seems to stand out: It takes time to nurture a marriage. We have to care enough to carve out time for each other even if that means sacrificing something else on the agenda.

The Lord has blessed me with a loving Christian husband. Lynn is the spiritual leader of our household, and I know he loves me not only because he tells me but because he sacrifices time for me. He's a busy attorney, overprogrammed with appointments and obligations, but I'll never forget the day he shoved all that aside because he knew I needed him.

I had entered a very personal story in a writing contest sponsored by a national publication. I felt led by the Lord to enter this contest, and through the months of waiting, I kept receiving affirmations that I would win. Perhaps because those kinds of affirmations don't come often in my life, I felt a special peace and confidence I hadn't felt before. Finally the day dawned when the results were to be announced, but I didn't receive a letter or phone call. By early afternoon, Lynn could stand the suspense no longer and called the magazine's editorial offices. They read him the list of winners, and my name was not among them. He called me and gently broke the news. He sensed my immediate disappointment, not only that I hadn't won but that I had so misunderstood the Lord's will. It was midafternoon, and he had a busy schedule. But he drove home to be with me when I needed him most. He was there to share my pain.

Looking back, I realize the pain passed quickly, but his gesture will always be vivid in my memory. He communicated his love by the sacrifice of his time.

Like all couples we can go days, sometimes longer, without an intimate, personal conversation. We get bogged down in house maintenance and parental discussions. We both begin to feel dry and irritable, and know it's time for dinner out alone together or better yet, one of our overnight escapes. Overnight escapes can either be planned or spur-of-the-moment, like last Christmas vacation. Winter storms had kept us all housebound for three days. I'd had my fill of wet mittens, drippy boots, and half-full cups of cold cocoa when a former baby-sitter, home from college, stopped by on Friday afternoon. She sensed the seriousness of my cabin fever and offered to stay with the kids. I met Lynn downtown after work, and we checked into a hotel near his office.

When we can't afford a dinner or weekend escape, I settle for a walk together in the evening. I know couples who regularly have lunch or breakfast out together one day a week, and it is a scheduled priority on their calendars.

Longer vacations together are more difficult to plan but worth the effort. One couple told us about going back to the island where they had spent their honeymoon sixteen years earlier. They even splurged on a romantic day of solitude when they were boated to their own private little island for the day. The boat delivered them to the beach early in the morning with a picnic basket and came back after sunset to pick them up.

"It's nice to discover again why you married this person in the first place," this mother of two preteens told me after their ten-day trip. "Only time away alone allows us to rediscover that."

As romantic as it sounds, I admit I have a hard time getting far away from our three children because I worry. We recently planned a five-day trip, and my anticipation was marred by my dumb worries: Will the kids be okay?; Will the baby-sitter use good judgment?; and What if . . . ? My concerns were a classic example of not letting go. It took me about twenty-four hours to deprogram myself from my role as mother and focus instead on my role as wife. We returned after a refreshing break from our routines at home and realized our children also benefited from the experience. They pulled together as siblings while we were gone and coped with responsibilities better than when we're home to assume those responsibilities. I think they developed a sense of security from knowing that we like to go away together. "The best thing I can do for my children is to love my wife," a father told me.

Friendships outside the home also need to be nurtured. We all know that good friendships don't just happen. They take time and sometimes sacrifice, but they are worth the effort. Friends sustain us when we're down; they come to our aid when we're in need; and they enlarge our circles so we don't become so family-centered that we have no other outlets. For the most part, our good friends will be around even after our children leave home, so they are a good investment.

I have one friend who sent her last one off to college several months ago and faced all the classic emotions of the empty-nest syndrome. She was extremely lonely, but a solid group of friends pulled her through. They cared. They took her out to lunch. They took her on a trip. They helped her redefine her goals and encouraged her to get a job. One even dropped everything to spend a day with her, riding up and down elevators in tall buildings to help her overcome her fear of heights and gain new confidence. That's a true friend.

NURTURE OUTSIDE INTERESTS

As our children grow, we have to invest our time wisely in outside interests that challenge us and improve our self-image in a way that is separate from parenting. As our lifestyle patterns change, we have to seek new outlets to develop neglected gifts. Our children's independence gives us added freedoms that nudge us into new directions. Preschool, all-day-long school, and freedom from getting baby-sitters and chauffeuring children give us the chance to spread our wings.

For women, one of the major milestones of independence comes when the youngest child goes off to school. If a mother hasn't been working, she finds herself faced with freedom that is sometimes frightening.

Sandra Day O'Connor, U.S. Supreme Court Justice, stayed home with her children when they were young but resumed her career when they started school. Then she went on to reach the height of success in her profession.

For women who don't know what direction to seek, many counseling centers offer something called an "interest inventory," a simple quiz that helps determine areas of aptitude and interest.

I have a friend who took a self-declared sabbatical after her last child trotted off to school. She resisted the temptation to jump into lots of activities quickly and refused requests to chair committees or join boards. She took the whole year off to decide what she wanted to do and gave the venture credibility by assigning a significant title to this important period in her life.

A final way we prepare for separation from our children is to make the most of the moments we have with them. That may sound contradictory, but it is not. If we make the most of the moments we have now, if we squeeze all the joy out of parenting, if we build a rich storehouse of memories, we will pass out of this era prepared and excited to seize upon the potential of the next.

CHAPTER 12

Fuzzy Release

"There is time for everything, and a season for every activity under heaven: a time to be born and a time to die, a time to plant and a time to uproot" (Eccl. 3:1–2). It is time to uproot.

We've anticipated this moment for years sometimes with fear, sometimes with joy. It is the moment of final release. The eaglet is ready to fly. The ship is ready to sail. The apron string is ready to be cut. It's a dramatic, meaningful, life–altering milestone.

There's only one problem. No one seems to know when the moment occurs. There is no ceremony, no retirement party for parents, no picture for the scrapbook that marks the moment the final cord is cut. After all these years of preparation, the final release is fuzzy and undefined.

Maybe that's our fault. Even though our job changes, we don't even get a title change. "Once a parent, always a parent," I heard one woman say. It reminded me of the grandmotherly lady who gently took my arm in the checkout line at the grocery store when I was overdue with our first child. She must have understood my impatience and fatigue.

"Your first?" she questioned, motioning to my balloon belly. I nodded. "Enjoy these last few days," she advised with a knowing smile. "You will never again be as free as you are right now. Once you have children, no matter how old they are or where they live, you will always be concerned about them."

Three children and many years later, I understand what she meant that day. We let go of our children one by one. We finish parenting. But our feelings for them never change. Only our responsibilities do.

Maybe the fuzzy release is the fault of our culture. We have no structure that clearly sets children on their own at a certain moment. We have no rituals or traditional rites of passage. In the past, parent-child separation began earlier and proceeded more slowly and smoothly with greater continuity between adolescent and adult responsibilities. In an agrarian society, children assumed more responsibilities earlier in life. They may have married earlier but they moved next door instead of halfway across the country. Often they continued to work within the family structure. They still came for the traditional Sunday dinners and counted on each other for support. Separation was less traumatic.

In our times, release is so fuzzy that even parents and children don't agree when it occurs. In a recent study, a group of eighteen-year-olds and their parents were asked if the adolescents were independent. The majority of youths answered that they were. The majority of parents answered they were not.[1]

On the other hand, maybe the fuzzy release is the children's fault. We don't know when they are gone because they keep coming back. For years they're half in and half out. Some, now called "nesters," move back home after months or years on their own.

One father assumed he was cutting the final cord when he left his eighteen-year-old daughter at her college dormitory on the west coast, halfway across the country from their home. Four years later, he realized that was not the final cord. After her graduation, she returned home for a brief visit, packed up the contents of her bedroom, loaded her car like a moving van, and pulled out of the driveway—alone—to go to a job in Washington, D.C.

"This time it's different," he reported a few days later, emotion still quivering in his voice. "This time she's really leaving."

A year later, he's not so sure again. "Emotionally she seems to need us more this year than she ever did in college. She is not surrounded by the same supportive group of friends and she calls home several times a week."

COLLEGE YEARS

Separation in our society generally takes place between the ages of eighteen and the early twenties. For many adolescents, these are college years, identified by the father of six grown children as "the most difficult in the separation process, at least for parents. "If the child is in college," he explains, "your financial investment in that child is greater than ever before. Yet your control and knowledge of what the child is doing is less than ever before. We found that period extremely frustrating, but the kids didn't. They were blissfully ignorant of the stress they were causing us."

This father went on to explain they did place one condition on their financial support. "We expected each of our children to get passing grades. If they didn't, we no longer paid their college tuition."

The college years include those famous visits home when a son or daughter breezes back into the same house with the same parents, and the same siblings after living in an entirely different environment with a different set of standards and total freedom. The scene almost always breeds disaster. It's the simple problem of differing expectations. The parents are hungry for descriptions of college life and anxious to make up for lost time. They visualize leisurely evenings around the dinner table and even plan menus of all the formerly favorite foods.

The student, on the other hand, who recently became a vegetarian and doesn't know how to break the news to his parents, visualizes mornings of sleeping late and evenings of catching up on all the news with his friends. Usually by the end of such a vacation, tempers have flared, feelings are wounded, and everyone is ready for the goodbyes.

"I expected a warm, affectionate daughter who missed home, and what I got was a young lady who didn't want her parents to interfere with her life anymore," one mother said after her daughter's first visit home.

A daughter reported, "My parents tried to parent too much when I went home. Suddenly after being totally on my own for three months, I had a curfew and obligations."

Like the rebellion of the high school student, much of this conflict melts away through the college years as the student grows more confident and secure in his or her independence. The parents' challenge at this time is to let go of outdated expectations and minimize the confrontations on issues that are not morally-threatening or life-threatening.

MARRIAGE

The marriage of a son or daughter is an obvious step in the letting-go process, but parents and offspring seem to differ on their emotional reactions to the occasion. One mother began feeling the tug when her future daughter-in-law started taking over some of her former privileges and responsibilities, like helping her son shop for new clothes or sewing a missing button on his shirt.

Do sons separate from parents more completely than daughters at marriage? "A daughter's a daughter all of her life; a son's a son 'til he takes him a wife," as the saying goes. Many parents believe that. "We still live in a maternal society," said one mother. "Our daughters remain closer to us than our sons. They are more likely to help us as we grow older." Yet "Dear Abby" columns are filled with descriptions of the struggle young marrieds go through in trying to please both sets of parents by evenly dividing holidays and vacations. For years, we stuffed down two Thanksgiving dinners a few hours apart, and Christmas was a marathon of house hopping.

"Dear Abby" also gets letters from the distraught wife who is tired of her husband going off to spend every Saturday with his mother in a neighboring town. It seems that how children separate from parents after marriage is a continuum of the pattern already established.

The father in one close-knit family claims he had no time to think about cutting the cord when he walked his twenty-two-year-old daughter down the aisle at her recent wedding in a large church before three hundred people. He was much too concerned about tripping on her gown. Yet a few days later in the quiet of their home, he felt the impact of her marriage because she and her new husband had moved to another state. Physical distance made the difference.

As a young woman, I felt a snip on my wedding day, but not the final snip. After weeks of hectic preparations and prenuptial activities, my husband and I left for our honeymoon immediately after the ceremony, and I remember feeling strangely sad at the distance between my family and me. They had worked so hard on our wedding plans, and I was totally cut off from them and unable to thank them. Believe it or not, I had a twinge of homesickness on our honeymoon.

After our June honeymoon, we spent the summer in Washington, D.C., but returned to the college in our hometown of Boulder, Colorado, where Lynn finished law school and I worked. Although we had our own apartment, it was almost as if we were playing house. Both our families lived in Boulder, and in all our minds, I believe, we didn't feel that much had changed in our relationships. If we joined them for dinner, we felt like children in their homes again. We felt certain obligations and responsibilities.

Our first Christmas, my whole family traveled to California to be with my sister and her family. For the first time, I didn't spend Christmas with them and I felt painfully left out. Even though I loved my husband and his family, I wallowed in self-pity most of the day.

It was not until a couple of years later, however, that I felt the most dramatic cut of a final cord. After Lynn graduated from law school, we boxed up all our worldly possessions, ready for a four-year stint in the Navy that would take us to Newport, Rhode Island, Chicago, and San Diego. We drove out of town at dusk headed east, and I watched the full moon rise over the horizon with tears in my eyes. "My parents and I will always watch the same moon in the same sky, but it will never be the same," I told myself. "From now on, we'll be separate." From my viewpoint, I cut the last cord that night.

And it never was the same. When we returned to make

our home in the same town four years later, we had a child of our own. We were finally a family with legitimate obligations to each other that took priority over our obligations to our parents.

During our four-year absence, Lynn and I had grown up and grown together. Undoubtedly physical separation had helped. We felt safely and happily emancipated. We were ready for the comfortable status of an adult-to-adult relationship with our parents partly because we now shared a common role as parents. Although today they sometimes slip back into the parental role of demands and expectations, and although we sometimes slip into the guilty child responses, generally we have untied the apron strings.

Does the addition of grandchildren cause a change in the parent-child relationship? Traditionally the first grandchild can cause one of two reactions: The new parents suddenly feel on equal footing with their parents as we did because we understand and appreciate the responsibilities and sacrifices of parenting; or the new baby causes friction between the generations as the grandparents criticize the way their child is raising their grandchild.

The period of fuzzy release may cause other problems for both parents and children. We may let go before the child is capable of coping or we may allow them to move back home after the release. Let's consider both situations.

PREMATURE RELEASE

Releasing a child who cannot cope may be disastrous, as it was in the well-known case of John Hinckley, Jr. At age twenty-five, John Jr. still did not seem ready to handle life's challenges. In fact, he begged his parents to let him come back home. He had dropped out of college and could not hold a job. His mother and father disagreed on how to handle the problem. As many parents might, they viewed his irresponsibility as a form of laziness but they also sensed some deeper problems.

"We didn't know what was wrong, but we knew something wasn't right," his mother remembers. Still, they bowed to the advice to get tough with young John and force him to become self-sufficient and financially independent. They said goodbye and closed the door.

One week later, John Jr. fired a bullet into the chest of President Reagan and catapulted himself and his family into worldwide news and the annals of history. Horrified and grief-stricken, his parents pieced the story together at the trial. His father touched all our hearts as he tearfully told the jurors, "I am the cause of John's tragedy." Referring to his decision to kick his son out of the house, he said, "I'm sure it was the greatest mistake of my life. We forced him out at a time he just couldn't cope."

Since then John Jr. has been declared innocent by reason of insanity, and his parents, deeply religious and committed to bringing good out of the tragedy, are devoting their lives to a better understanding of the mentally ill. They are touring the United States with a message to parents. "For heaven's sake, don't kick somebody out of the house when they can't cope," this father pleads.[2]

The meaning is clear. If your child can't cope, no matter what age, get help and take care of that child as long as he or she needs care. Need is the key word. A teenager with a serious, habitual drug problem or a mental problem needs help. And parents are still the most capable of finding that help.

NESTERS

Need of a different nature seems to be bringing other young people back home to roost in growing numbers across the country. They are called "nesters," a contemporary term that refers to young adults who move home or stay home to live with parents, probably due to the economic crunch.

Regardless of the reason, however, the situation sets up many new challenges and adjustments within the family. Some of these depend on whether the young adult is moving back home alone or with a spouse and children or whether other siblings are still living at home.

The situation always demands some forethought. First, the parents must consider their attitude about the living arrangement. They have a choice. Do they take the child back or do they insist he or she makes it alone? Some parents resist the arrangement, fearing their children will become too dependent if they move back home. Others believe like Robert Frost: "Home is the place where when you have to go there, they have to take you in."[3]

Parents should examine their motives for allowing or wanting their children to move back home. If a possessive mother looks forward to taking care of her child again or expects companionship through the arrangement, it's bound to cause conflicts.

Parent and child should discuss conditions of the living arrangement beforehand. What are the rules and expectations? Does the child contribute to room and board? If the child has a job, most parents insist on at least partial payments. If the child has no source of income, the parents may insist on a plan of action to assure that the child finds a job. This may include going back to school, getting specialized training, or simply searching for work. The parents may ask the child to contribute to the workload around the house: do some laundry, help clean, and fix one or two meals a week.

Does the child have complete freedom, or do the parents still have some authority? Maybe the child is responsible for his or her own decisions but agrees to abide by the family rules and value system, especially if younger brothers and sisters are still living at home.

If handled correctly, the nester situations can be a time of emotional and spiritual growth within a family, as parents and children learn to adjust and offer each other support in time of need. If handled incorrectly, the move home could make the adult child more dependent on the parents. At best, the nester period should be viewed as temporary, just another step in the journey toward independence.

ADULT–TO–ADULT FRIENDSHIP

After adolescents graduate from high school and leave home, our aim is to reach the plateau of a smoother adult-to-adult relationship with them. No longer should we try to nag, shape, and change them. Our parenting responsibilities are finished, which gives us a new freedom to build a friendship with them. Sometimes we don't see our children as friends until they have left home and returned, as Marilee Zdenek describes in her book *Splinters in My Pride*.

> *It was hard when you went away—*
> *For how was I to know*
> *The serendipity of letting go*
> *Would be seeing you come home again*
> *And meeting in a new way*
> *Woman to woman—*
> *Friend to friend.*[4]

Consider the potential for such a friendship. After all, we know our children better than anyone else. We made memories with them; we were around when their personalities were being molded.

That many parents and children never reach this plateau of friendship is evidenced by the parent-child relationships we see in the adults around us. Watch the response when a friend announces his or her mother is coming to town for a two-week visit. The news is almost always met with a series of automatic groans to express sympathy for the endurance of such a struggle.

A 1981 survey of 2,600 adults showed that 89 percent of them claim they suffer from long-term strained relationships with their parents. Nearly half of them complain their parents still are overprotective.[5] This study tells us we aren't releasing our grown children, even as our parents didn't release us. And we aren't nurturing adult-to-adult friendships with them.

What is standing in our way? Maybe it's our little habits that subtly tell them we are still the parents and they are still the children. Think of the ways we criticize or judge them. Before we voice any disapproval to our adult children, we should ask ourselves: Will it do any good?; Will it have a positive effect? If the answer is no, the action is obvious. We should keep our mouths closed.

"Parents who once firmly directed their children's lives, parents who once firmly voiced disapproval of their children's style of living, often come to a point where love and appreciation for respect and kindness win out over attitudes of judgment," writes Evelyn Bence in *Leaving Home*.[6]

Another stumbling block to our adult friendships with our children is more nebulous. Do we allow them to be adults in our presence? Chelsea in the movie *On Golden Pond*, felt grown up and capable except when she was around her parents. Then she felt like a little girl again, struggling to please her parents and meet their expectations, especially her father's.

You Can't Go Home Again the title of a play tells us, and the message applies. Our children can't comfortably come home again until and unless we treat them as adults. Granted, it's a two-way street. They must gain the confidence and maturity to feel like adults, but we must encourage that confidence. As a young adult, one way I knew I was reaching that level of adult friendship with my parents was that I could begin calling their friends by their first names. It was a signal I was coming of age.

BREEDING GUILT

A major stumbling block to healthy adult relationships with our children is a subtle but powerful one. It is the way we continue to produce guilt in our adult children. Breeding guilt is a form of bribery, an attempt to manipulate or control our adult children's behavior. The tactics may vary, but the results are always the same: the adult child feels guilty because he or she did not please the parents, just as in childhood when doing something wrong made the child fearful of losing the parents' love. The adult children recognize this helpless childlike feeling their parents produce, but they don't know how to deal with it.

Take this example, a phone call I made to my mother when I was in college.

"Hello," I said brightly when she answered.

"Well, hello, I thought you forgot my phone number," she said sarcastically. "It's been a long time. . . ."

"Oh . . . I've been busy," I stammered defensively, trying to make excuses.

Instead of being happy to hear from me, she was scolding me for not calling sooner. I felt the "naughty child" response, and for the rest of the conversation, I was on the defensive. Her tactic didn't make me want to call more often, which was her intent. It made me vow not to call for a long time. I was angry and frustrated. Obviously, I didn't please my mother. But I hope I've learned one thing from this familiar experience. When my grown children call, I will be honest rather than sarcastic. I will tell them I am happy to hear from them. Maybe that will make them want to call more often.

A common manipulative gesture is giving a gift with strings attached. Usually it's a bribe for attention. "One can dominate others through gifts," Paul Tournier says in *The Meaning of a Gift.*[7] The gift of the plane ticket home every Christmas carries with it the obligation of time and the sacrifice of establishing one's own family traditions. What if the child asks for the same plane trip home in March instead? Is the offer good only if it fulfills the parents' expectations of what Christmas should be?

The gift of money often comes with strings attached. "Our son and his wife needed money because they were broke, and the rent was due," one father recalls. "We gave them money, expecting they would use it for the rent. They didn't. Instead, they went out and bought something we didn't think they needed. We were upset for months. Finally, we reached the conclusion that if we chose to give them money, we couldn't dictate how that money should be spent. It has to be a gift, given by choice. And we have to respect their choice of how to spend it."

Letting go hinges on our ability to give up our outmoded expectations. "When I was a child, I talked like a child, I thought like a child, I reasoned like a child. When I became a man, I put childish ways behind me" (1 Cor. 13:11). This verse applies to us as parents as much as to our children. We mature through the seasons of life. We give up inappropriate roles or behavior. We stop parenting through control and manipulation.

We give advice or gifts out of concern for our children's

well-being, not to continue our position of power over them. We admit that we make mistakes, and they make mistakes, like forgetting to call, and we forgive openly and easily. We don't depend on them to satisfy our needs. We encourage and acknowledge their freedom.

PARENTAL GUILT

There's another totally different side to the subject of guilt in the parent-child relationship. This is the guilt a parent feels when a child does not grow up the way the parent had hoped or expected. This is a paralyzing, painful guilt that can render us incapable of coping with any of the Lord's future challenges in life.

I remember the words of a heartbroken mother who had discovered her adult daughter had chosen to become a homosexual. She was grief-stricken and guilt-ridden. How did I go wrong? What did I do, or what didn't I do? She agonized over those questions until with help she began to understand that when you lose control, you give up responsibility. She had long ago lost the ability to control her grown daughter, so she was no longer responsible for the choices that daughter made.

"Train up a child in the way he should go, and when he is old, he will not turn from it" (Prov. 22:6). That is a probability not a promise. We are not totally responsible for the outcome of our training. We are only responsible for training. We don't control the temperament with which our children were born. We don't entirely control their environment, especially their peer group as they grow up. We do not control the will of our children; they have free will as we do.

If we disagree with their behavior, we don't condone it, support it, or bail out our children. And we don't claim responsibility and later guilt for it either. We don't send money to support a son's drug habit. We don't allow a daughter to use the bedroom in our home to sleep with the boyfriend who shares her apartment in another city.

We are responsible for their training when they are young and dependent upon us, but they are responsible for their choices and actions in adolescence and adulthood.

Surely we make mistakes in child rearing. All parents do. We wish we had the biblical knowledge then that we do now; we might have done things differently. But the Lord forgives us and promises to restore those years we feel we wasted. "I will restore to you the years which the swarming locust has eaten" (Joel 2:25 RSV).

After our children are grown and gone, we still have power and influence in their lives. We offer them support through our continuing unconditional and forgiving love, as the father does with the prodigal son. And we continue to pray for them unceasingly, as David prayed for his own son Solomon just before Solomon was made king. David, a father who made mistakes in his parenting, feared his son was inexperienced for the task that he faced. David prayed, "Grant to Solomon my son that with a whole heart he may keep thy commandments, thy testimonies, and thy statutes, performing all" (1 Chron. 29:19 RSV). As they grow up and leave our homes, we continue to pray for them, as Joyce Landorf says, "until they put a lily in our hands and close the lid."[8]

CHAPTER 13

Soaring

We raise our children to leave us. Why, then, does it hurt when they go? Why is the empty house so suddenly lonely and the silence so deafening?

Parents face a period of adjustment in this season of life, a time often filled with conflicting, confusing emotions. The loss we feel is real. In fact, we may experience the stages of grief common to those mourning a death because mourning is a normal reaction to a loss whether it be death, divorce, or separation. On the Holmes-Rahe Stress test, losing a close family member rates close to the top of major stresses in life. Loss means change in lifestyle, and change usually causes pain.

Hospice, a national organization that helps families deal with death and dying, offers support to people in bereavement. They gently assure a grieving person that his or her feelings are normal and healthy, and they find that the expression of those feelings gets the person through the grieving process more quickly and comfortably.

"We allowed ourselves to grieve when our final child left the nest," one mother confided to me. "We experienced a sense of deep loss and all the pain that goes with it, but I know we've come through it more prepared for God's next challenge because of our grieving process."

In other words, we need to acknowledge our feelings in

response to the separation. We may feel depressed, confused, listless, and unmotivated. These feelings are real but temporary. There will be brighter moments, even rewards, ahead.

"I moped around the house for two weeks after our youngest left for college, but I didn't cry," one mother told me. "On Friday afternoon of the second week, I was wheeling the shopping cart through the grocery store and stopped in the cereal section. Suddenly it hit me. I didn't need to buy Wheat Chex anymore and I stood there crying for a long time. But then I came home to a clean house with no dirty laundry, and my husband and I had a great weekend of freedom alone together. And I liked it!"

Is the empty nest adjustment more difficult for the mother or the father? For years, we have assumed the adjustment is more painful for the mother, especially if she had stayed home to care for her family through the years. She may find herself with nothing to do and little self-confidence to seek a change.

But the women's movement, as controversial as it has been, has sparked a change in this area over the last several years. Fewer and fewer women are reaching the empty-nest season with no preparation for fulfillment beyond motherhood. More women seem to have a healthy attitude about the opportunities and options available to them in this period of increased freedom.

Fathers, on the other hand, may be feeling more grief than previously thought. Young fathers are taking an increased interest in child-rearing responsibilities, an attitude change that seems to be affecting fathers of every age. Many fathers describe feeling older during the empty-nest season and more nostalgic about the loss of chances to make memories with their children. They regret the busyness of their lives that robbed them of opportunities to spend more time with their children.

One father said God had the time frame mixed up. His job required his maximum time and energy when his kids were young and needed him most. Nearly twenty years later when his job-related pressures and responsibilities slackened off, his children were leaving home.

The season of the empty nest may coincide with other life-altering experiences. For women, it may be menopause. For both men and women, it may be the midlife crisis, a more defined and recognized period of life when a man or woman confronts the passage of time and reexamines the values governing that life. It may trigger the need for a move to a smaller house or motivate a remodeling job, turning children's former bedrooms into offices, guest rooms, or even a duplex rental unit. All these changes can cause stress.

The empty nest may also coincide with the death or impending death of one or both of our own parents. "I feel tugged by both generations," explained one mother. "My son is packing up to go off to college, and my father is dying of cancer. I'm facing a double loss; I feel confused and even angry."

As our own parents get older, we examine our relationship with them and in turn our relationship with our own children. "Although I'm sure he loved me, my father never showed much affection," one father lamented. "Now that my son is ready to leave home, I'm afraid I haven't hugged him or told him I love him often enough."

With older parents we also face a role reversal that causes an emotional adjustment. Instead of being taken care of, we begin to take care of them in subtle little ways. We drive the car instead of letting them drive. We remind them to take a sweater in case the evening gets chilly. We help them decide what to order from the menu and even cut their meat. If this role reversal coincides with the emptying of the nest, we feel a keener awareness of the passing of time in our lives.

The marriage relationship usually undergoes a change during the empty-nest season. Suddenly, we set only two places at the table and have more time to think about this person who shares the pork chops.

"When children leave there is more time to notice and confront each other. The buffer and distraction of children is no longer present. Often the romance and passion of the earlier years are gone, the adhesive that is very much needed but is so difficult to generate once again," writes H. Norman Wright in *Seasons of a Marriage*.[1]

Then again, we can turn this challenge into an opportunity. Sometimes God shakes up our categories to motivate us to grow and change. Many parents on the other side of the empty-nest adjustment give glowing reports of their new lives. "When the last child leaves home, a new emotion sets in," claims Charles Shedd. "ECSTASY!"[2]

"This is a marvelous time of life!" Jill Briscoe enthusiastically tells a group of women at a seminar and then encourages, "You want to go back to work? Super! The working world needs vibrant Christian women being light in dark places."

Like many major changes in our lives, we can choose our attitude of response. We can dwell on the negative or focus on the positive. Finally, I can trade the station wagon in on a sportier car! Finally, we have leftovers in the house again. Finally, the public service bill is down and so is the volume on the stereo; even the choice of music is ours alone. We can be impulsive: make dinner or choose not to make dinner; or go away for a weekend on a moment's notice.

The bathroom is clean, and the evenings give us stretches of time for ourselves. There is noticed progress in the adjustment to life without them. "I'm so proud of myself when I have to look up his phone number," one mother happily reported shortly after her youngest moved out.

Maybe it's time for a weekend marriage seminar. Eventually it will be time to put all that memorabilia into a scrapbook for each child, a healthy way to absorb the nostalgic feelings. It's time to look back with pride not regret.

Erma Bombeck, known for her wit and sensitivity as a wife and mother, compares raising a child to flying a kite. She says we spend a lifetime trying to get them off the ground, running with them, trying again and again.

Finally they are airborne: they need more string and you keep letting it out. But with each twist of the ball of twine, there is a sadness that goes with joy. The kite becomes more distant, and you know it won't be long before that beautiful creature will snap the lifeline that binds you together and will soar as it is meant to soar, free and alone. Only then do you know that you did your job.[3]

The blessings of release will be more than we ever imagined. Hannah, who was barren for so many years, gave her only son Samuel to the Lord. In return, she was richly blessed with five more children. And Samuel grew to serve God mightily. What better reward could a parent receive? Mary released her son Jesus in order that he might fulfill God's plan for his life. Consider her rewards.

The blessings come in different packages. One mother, Joan Mills, writes that she discovered the best part of parenting when her grown children left home. "The generations smile at one another, as if exchanging congratulations. The children are no longer children. The parents are awed to discover adults," and that, she concludes, "is the final, firmest bonding; the goal and the reward."[4]

When our children grow up and leave home, our parenting responsibilities are over. We have trained them up, loved them dearly, and stirred up the nest to release them. We will always love them, always pray for them, but our work is done. As Christians, however, we are taught that the end is always a beginning. This is the end of an era but the beginning of an opportunity to start a new adventure with the Lord.

It is a time to soar freely.

NOTES

CHAPTER 2
1. John White, *Parents in Pain* (Downers Grove, Ill: InterVarsity Press, 1979), 164–165, as quoted in H. Norman Wright, *Seasons of a Marriage* (Ventura, Calif.: Regal Books, 1982), 94.

CHAPTER 3
1. Kahlil Gibran, *The Prophet* (New York: Alfred A. Knopf, 1923), 17.
2. Catherine Marshall, *To Live Again* (Charlotte, N.C.: Commission Press, 1957), 119.
3. David Elkind, *The Hurried Child* (Reading, Mass.: Addison-Wesley, 1981), 30.
4. Erma Bombeck, *Motherhood, The Second Oldest Profession* (New York: McGraw-Hill, 1983), 30.
5. Michael V. Bloom, *Adolescent-Parental Separation* (New York: Gardner Press, 1980), 53.
6. Phyllis Theroux, "What Your Kids Really Want," *American Home* (May 1977), 37.
7. Bloom, 23.

CHAPTER 4
1. Margie M. Lewis, "Hope for the Hurting Parent" (Arcadia, Calif.: Focus on the Family, 1983), booklet excerpted from *The Hurting Parent* (Grand Rapids: Zondervan, 1980).
2. Nancy P. McConnell, "Thoughts on Motherhood" (Colorado Springs: Current, Inc., 1983).
3. " 'Parent Burnout': Latest Sign of Today's Stresses," interview with Joseph Procaccini in *U.S. News & World Report* (7 March 1983), 76–77.
4. James C. Dobson, "Setting Your Adolescent Free" (Arcadia, Calif.: Focus on the Family), abstracted from James C. Dobson, *The Strong-Willed Child* (Wheaton, Ill.: Tyndale House Publishers, 1978).
5. Foster Cline, "What Shall We Do with This Kid?" in Parent Education Seminar, Boulder, Colorado, 1982.
6. Anonymous, "Our Teenage Daughter Ran Away" in the series "My Problem and How I Solved It," *Good Housekeeping* (January 1984), 28–34.
7. Tim Brennan, Delbert S. Elliott, and David Huizinga, *The Social Psychology of Runaways* (Lexington, Mass.: D.C. Heath & Co., Lexington Books, 1978), 160.
8. Foster W. Cline, *Parent Education Text* (Evergreen, Colo.: Evergreen Consultants in Human Behavior, 1982), 23.

CHAPTER 5
1. Larry Christenson, *The Christian Family* (Minneapolis: Bethany House Publishers, 1970), 64–65.

2. Hughes Mearns, "Every Child Has a Gift," *Keys to Happiness* (Pleasantville, N.Y.: Reader's Digest Association, 1955), 223–26.
3. Evelyn Bence, *Leaving Home* (Philadelphia: Bridgebooks, Westminster Press, 1952), 153.

CHAPTER 6
1. Charles R. Swindoll, "Releasing the Reins," sound cassette in "Christian Family Living" series (Fullerton, Calif.: Insight for Living, 1981).
2. Dietrich Bonhoeffer, *Letters and Papers from Prison*, as quoted in *Leaving Home* (Philadelphia: Bridgebooks, Westminister Press, 1952), 31.
3. Kevin Leman, *Parenthood Without Hassles—Well Almost* (Irvin, Calif.: Harvest House), as quoted in "Dear Abby," *Daily Camera* newspaper (13 January 1981).
4. Dolores Curran, *Traits of a Healthy Family* (Minneapolis: Winston Press, 1983), 166, 184.

CHAPTER 7
1. "What's Happening to American Families?" *Better Homes and Gardens* (July 1983), 15–16; (August 1983), 24.
2. Phyllis Theroux, "What Your Kids Really Want," *American Home* (May 1977), 37.
3. James C. Dobson, "Values in the Home" (Arcadia, Calif.: Focus on the Family, 1982), 1.
4. Larry Christenson, *The Christian Family* (Minneapolis: Bethany House Publishers, 1970), 165.
5. Ibid., 55.

CHAPTER 8
1. Bernice Weissbourd, "Declarations of Dependence," *Parents* (January 1983), 70.
2. Mary White, "Developing Your Child's Devotional Life" (Arcadia, Calif.: Focus on the Family, 1982), booklet excerpted from Mary White, *Successful Family Devotions* (Colorado Springs: Navigators Press, 1981).

CHAPTER 9
1. Larry Christenson, *The Christian Family* (Minneapolis: Bethany House Publishers, 1970), 151.
2. Mary White, "Developing Your Child's Devotional Life" (Arcadia, Calif.: Focus on the Family, 1982), booklet excerpted from Mary White, *Successful Family Devotions* (Colorado Springs: Navigators Press, 1981).

CHAPTER 10
1. Michael V. Bloom, *Adolescent-Parental Separation* (New York: Gardner Press, 1980), 42.
2. Jay Kesler, *Too Big to Spank* (Ventura, Calif.: Regal Books, 1978), 89.
3. Tim Brennan, Delbert S. Elliott, and David Huizinga, *The Social Psychology of Runaways* (Lexington, Mass.: D.C. Heath & Co., Lexington Books, 1978), 156–58.
4. H. G. Ginott, *Between Parent and Teenager* (New York: Macmillan, 1969), 111.
5. Interview with Delbert S. Elliott, behavioral researcher.
6. "The Christian Family," *New Life Magazine* (January 1983), 7.

CHAPTER 11
1. H. Norman Wright, *Seasons of a Marriage* (Ventura Calif.: Regal Books, 1982), 90.
2. Marguerite Beecher and Willard Beecher, *Parents on the Run?* as quoted in *Dr. Dobson Answers Your Questions* (Wheaton, Ill: Tyndale House Publishers, 1982), 206.
3. Joyce Landorf, *Changepoints* (Old Tappan, N.J.: Fleming H. Revell, 1981), 54.
4. Anne Morrow Lindbergh, *Gift from the Sea* (New York: Pantheon, 1955), introduction.

CHAPTER 12
1. Michael V. Bloom, *Adolescent-Parental Separation* (New York: Gardner Press, 1980), 73.
2. Facts and quotes compiled from newspaper reports, 1982.
3. Robert Frost, "The Death of the Hired Hand," *Robert Frost's Poems* (New York: Washington Square Press, 1960), 165.
4. Marilee Zdenek, *Splinters in My Pride* (Waco Tex: Word Books, 1979), part 1 reprinted in Charles Swindoll *Make Up Your Mind About the Issues of Life,* (Portland, Ore.: Multnomah, 1981), 34.
5. Focus on the Family Reader's Poll, Arcadia, California, 1981.
6. Evelyn Bence, *Leaving Home* (Philadelphia: Bridgebooks, Westminster Press, 1952), 158.
7. Ibid., 157.
8. Joyce Landorf, *Changepoints* (Old Tappan, N.J.: Fleming H. Revell, 1981), 157.

CHAPTER 13
1. H. Norman Wright, *Seasons of a Marriage* (Ventura, Calif.: Regal Books, 1982), 55.
2. Charles Shedd, "How to Stay in Love," part of film series "Fun in Marriage Workshop," Cinema Associates.
3. Erma Bombeck, "At Wit's End," Field Newspaper Syndicate (2 May 1978).

4. Joan Mills, "When My Grown Children Left Home" in Focus on the Family newsletter (November 1983), reprinted from *Reader's Digest* (January 1981).